Disruptive Technologies and Business Innovation: IoT in Perspective

Edited by

Mohammed Majeed
Department of Marketing, Tamale Technical University
Tamale, Ghana

Jonas Yomboi
St. John's Integrated SHTS, Navrongo
Ghana

Sulemana Ibrahim
Department of Marketing
Tamale Technical University, Tamale, Ghana

&

Esther Asiedu
Ghana Communication Technology University
Accra, Ghana

Disruptive Technologies and Business Innovation: IoT in Perspective

Editors: Mohammed Majeed, Jonas Yomboi, Sulemana Ibrahim and Esther Asiedu

ISBN (Online): 978-981-5322-88-0

ISBN (Print): 978-981-5322-89-7

ISBN (Paperback): 978-981-5322-90-3

Published by Bentham Science Publishers Pte. Ltd. Singapore. All Rights Reserved.

First published in 2024.

need for a court order if at any point you breach any terms of this License Agreement. In no event will any delay or failure by Bentham Science Publishers in enforcing your compliance with this License Agreement constitute a waiver of any of its rights.

3. You acknowledge that you have read this License Agreement, and agree to be bound by its terms and conditions. To the extent that any other terms and conditions presented on any website of Bentham Science Publishers conflict with, or are inconsistent with, the terms and conditions set out in this License Agreement, you acknowledge that the terms and conditions set out in this License Agreement shall prevail.

Bentham Science Publishers Pte. Ltd.
80 Robinson Road #02-00
Singapore 068898
Singapore
Email: subscriptions@benthamscience.net

BENTHAM SCIENCE

CONTENTS

PREFACE i

LIST OF CONTRIBUTORS ii

CHAPTER 1 INTERNET OF THINGS IN MARKETING: AN INTRODUCTION 1
Mohammed Majeed, Vijaya Kittu Manda, Sulemana Ibrahim and *Esther Asiedu*
INTRODUCTION 1
LITERATURE 3
    Internet of Things (IoTs) 3
    Internet of Things in Marketing 4
BENEFITS OF IOT IN MARKETING 8
    Targeted Advertising 8
    Added Value and Competitive Advantage 9
    Facilitated Innovation 9
    The Optimization of Processes and Operations for Enhanced Efficiency 9
    The IoTs Aids Equipment Maintenance Needs 10
    The Act of Disrupting Business Models 10
    Monitoring 10
    Digitalized Factory 11
    Enhance Prospects for Corporate Growth and Financial Gain 11
    Intelligent Security Systems 11
    Delivery Tracking 12
    A Deeper Understanding of Consumer Behavior 12
    Enhancement of Customer Service and Insight (Experience) 12
    Enhance Business Operations and Promote Workplace Safety 12
    Enhance Levels of Production and Augment Competence 13
    Assistance is Requested in Conducting an Analysis of Consumer Behavior 13
    Reducing Operational Expenses 13
    Enhancing the Capabilities of Intelligent Device Applications 14
    IoT in the Near Future 14
    Implication 15
CONCLUSION 16
REFERENCES 17

CHAPTER 2 PRODUCT AND THE INTERNET OF THINGS (IOT) 19
Jonas Yomboi, Mohammed Majeed and *Esther Asiedu*
INTRODUCTION 19
LITERATURE 21
    IoT 21
    Product 21
    Product and Internet of Things (IoT) 22
    Components 23
    Social Media 24
    Warranty 25
PLM 25
    Packaging 26
    Customer Engagement 28
    Innovation 28
    Customer Empowerment 29
    Exposing the Utilization of the Product 29
    Quality Control 29

Experience 29
Demand 30
Brand 30
Quality of Products and Services 31
The Characteristics/Features and Capabilities 32
Product Style 32
The Factors of Efficiency and Accessibility 33
The Provision of After-sales Service 33
The Level of User-friendliness 33
The Product Line Length within the Realm of IoT Commerce 34
Various Stock-keeping Units (SKUs) 34
The Fulfillment of Customer Demand 35
The Breadth of Firms' Portfolio 35
Implications 35
CONCLUSION 36
REFERENCES 36

CHAPTER 3 INTERNET OF THINGS (IOT) AND PRICING 39
S. Jayadatta, Mohammed Majeed, Seidu Alhassan and *Sulemana Anas*
INTRODUCTION 39
LITERATURE 41
IoT in Marketing 41
Price/Pricing 41
Price Internet of Things 42
ROI 43
Discounts 43
Subscription 43
Connivance and Deceit 43
Margins 44
Goodness of the Data 44
Means of Exchange 44
Sensors 44
Market-Based Pricing 44
Skimming the Market with Prices 45
Competitive Pricing 45
High-End Costs 45
Pricing Based on Value 45
Penetration Pricing 45
Pricing based on Psychology 46
Geographical Pricing (Pricing Based on Location) 46
Prices Determined by Market Forces 46
IoT for New Prices Introduction 47
Bundles Pricing 47
IoT and the Future of Pricing 47
Implications 47
CONCLUSION 48
REFERENCES 48

CHAPTER 4 PROMOTION AND THE INTERNET OF THINGS 50
Mohammed Majeed, Ibrahim Osman and *Abdul-Fatahi Abdul-Karim Abubakar*
INTRODUCTION 50
LITERATURE 52

IoT 52
Promotion 53
Promotion Internet of Things (PmIoTs) 54
Contextual Segmentation 56
Community Influencers 56
In-Store Advertising 56
Reward Programs 56
Location-Based Advertising 57
Internet/Digital Marketing 57
Personalization Engines 57
Public Relations 58
Personalized Emails 58
Intent-Based Advertising 59
Dynamic Website Content 59
CRM Ads 59
Personalized Advertisements with Beacons 59
Interactive Advertising 60
Print 60
Unveiling Consumer Intentions 60
Sales Promotion 61
Radio 61
Personal Selling 61
The Role of Email Marketing in IoT Commerce 62
SEO 62
Direct Marketing 62
The Facilitation of Public Relations Communication 63
The phenomenon of Increasingly Discerning Consumers 63
IMC 63
The Complexity of the Media Mix 64
Enables the Promotion of Products or Services 64
The Topic of Discussion Pertains to In-Store Promotions 64
Enhancing Consumer Awareness with Transparent Product Information 65
Conventional Advertising 65
The Advantages of Websites 65
Social Media 66
Television (TV) 66
Implications 66
CONCLUSION 67
REFERENCES 67

CHAPTER 5 INTERNET OF THINGS AND MARKETING MIX 69
Mohammed Majeed
INTRODUCTION 69
LITERATURE 70
IoT 70
Marketing Mix (7Ps) 71
IOTS AND MARKETING MIX 73
Products 73
Pricing 75
Distribution 77
Promotion 78

People 78

Physicals 79

Processes 79

Implications 79

CONCLUSION 79

REFERENCES 81

CHAPTER 6 PLACE/DISTRIBUTION AND THE INTERNET OF THINGS 82

Mohammed Majeed, Ahmed Sakara, Alhassan Yahaya and *Mohammed Abdul-Basit Fuseini*

INTRODUCTION 82

LITERATURE 84

IoT 84

Place/Distribution 85

Place/Distribution Internet of Things (DIoT) 85

HOW IS IOT USED IN DISTRIBUTION/PLACE 87

Retailing and E-Commerce 87

Factory of the Future or Smart Manufacturing 87

Prioritizing Health 88

Firm's Website 88

Temperature and Humidity Sensors 89

Aggregators 89

Optimize Operations 89

Supply Chain Sourcing 90

Mitigate the Occurrence of Theft 90

Specialty Stores 90

Big Data 91

Direct Sales 91

Supply Chain Planning 92

Business-to-business 92

IoT Commerce 93

The Implementation of Proactive Maintenance Strategies for Assets 94

Autonomous Cars and Drones 94

Radio Frequency Identification (RFID) 95

Global Positioning System (GPS) 95

The Provision of Instantaneous Notifications 95

Benefits of IoT for Place/SCM/Distribution 95

Implications 100

CONCLUSION 100

REFERENCES 101

CHAPTER 7 INTERNET OF THINGS IN MARKETING: THE CUSTOMER EXPERIENCE 103

Salifu Shani, Mohammed Majeed, Parag Shukla and *Sofia Devi Shamurailatpam*

INTRODUCTION 104

LITERATURE 105

CX 105

Internet of Things 106

INTERNET OF THINGS IMPACTING ON CUSTOMER EXPERIENCE 107

Optimized Usage of the Product 107

Enhanced Client Service 108

Enhancing the Quality of Products and Services 108

Enhanced Security 108

IoT for Quality 109
Sales Automation 109
Timely and Pertinent Offerings 109
Personalization 110
Enhancing the Quality of In-store Encounters 110
The Prompt and Efficient Resolution of Issues 110
IoT can Effectively Enhance Consumer Loyalty 111
The Provision of Outstanding Customer Support Services 111
Advertisements 111
Monitor the Movement of the Supply Chain 112
Accelerated Legal Claims 113
Improving Business Continuity 113
Trustworthy 113
IoT-enabled Devices 114
Real-Time Data 114
Implications 114
CONCLUSION 115
REFERENCES 116

CHAPTER 8 INTERNET OF THINGS, MARKETING, AND MARKET RESEARCH 118
Benjamin NiiBoye Oda, Bright Owusu Kwame, Banaba David Alaaba, Seidu
Alhassan and *Mohammed Abdul-Basit Fuseini*
INTRODUCTION 118
LITERATURE REVIEW 119
Internet of Things 119
Marketing and Market Research 119
Market Research 120
Marketing Research 121
Impact of IoT on Marketing Research 121
Pursuing Consumer Behavior 122
Experimentation 124
Projecting Consumer Behavior 124
Providing Customized Experiences 125
Interconnected and Secure Infrastructure 125
The Cloud and IoT go Hand in Hand 125
Old School Industries are the Pioneers of Adopting New Technologies 126
Hardware and Software 126
Security 126
Implications 127
CONCLUSION 127
REFERENCES 127

CHAPTER 9 SMART MANUFACTURING FOR FASHION FIRMS 129
Abas Sherifatu, Joana Akweley Zanu, Musah Bukari and *Eunice Acheampomaa*
Ameyaw
INTRODUCTION 130
LITERATURE 131
Smart Manufacturing 131
Type of Technologies Used in Smart Manufacturing 132
Connectivity 132
RFID 132
Robotics 132

Virtual Reality and Augmented Reality 133
Digital Twins 133
Internet of Things 133
Sensors 134
Computer-Assisted Design (CAD) System 134
Benefits of SM 134
The Future of Smart Manufacturing 135
CONCLUSION 136
REFERENCES 136

SUBJECT INDEX 138

PREFACE

In contemporary times, a widespread recognition of the significance of the Internet of Things (IoT) is evident among various stakeholders, including advertisers, marketers, and customers. The editors seek to enhance the knowledge of marketers and customers regarding IoT technology in order to optimize the utilization of data and customer-related information obtained from various web-connected devices. The book demonstrates the ways in which the IoT enriches the customer experience, supports the volume of data acquired through interconnected devices, and expands the range of analytics. The book presents a diverse array of marketing opportunities, encompassing enhanced sales strategies for existing products and services, the provision of highly tailored client experiences, and the possibility for innovation in the form of new products, services, research, and pricing. The IoT provides organizations with the ability to obtain real-time visibility into the actual functioning of their systems, hence enabling them to gain valuable information pertaining to many aspects, such as machine performance and marketing operations. The book endeavors to examine multiple facets of utilizing the Internet of Things for marketing purposes, delineate significant challenges, and provide possible remedies. Marketers have the opportunity to leverage the vast potential of the Internet of Things (IoT) in the future. Nevertheless, the current body of literature pertaining to marketing strategies for the IoT remains limited in scope and depth (Riyas et al., 2023). The book demonstrates the ways in which IoT is facilitating the growth of businesses and enhancing the attractiveness of their products and services to consumers. IoT facilitates global corporate connectivity and data sharing.

Mohammed Majeed
Department of Marketing, Tamale Technical University
Tamale, Ghana

Jonas Yomboi
St. John's Integrated SHTS, Navrongo
Ghana

Sulemana Ibrahim
Department of Marketing
Tamale Technical University, Tamale, Ghana

&

Esther Asiedu
Ghana Communication Technology University
Accra, Ghana

List of Contributors

Ahmed Sakara Department of Marketing, Tamale Technical University, Tamale, Ghana

Alhassan Yahaya Department of Marketing, Tamale Technical University, Tamale, Ghana

Abas Sherifatu Department of Graphic Communication Design Technology, Tamale Technical University, Tamale, Ghana

Abdul-Fatahi Abdul-Karim Abubakar Marketing Department, Tamale Technical University, Tamale, Ghana

Benjamin NiiBoye Oda Marketing Department, Tamale Technical University, Tamale, Ghana

Bright Owusu Kwame Marketing Department, Tamale Technical University, Tamale, Ghana

Banaba David Alaaba Marketing Department, Tamale Technical University, Tamale, Ghana

Eunice Acheampomaa Ameyaw Department of Graphic Communication Design Technology, Tamale Technical University, Tamale, Ghana

Esther Asiedu Ghana Communication Technology University, Accra, Ghana

Ibrahim Osman Marketing Department, Tamale Technical University, Tamale, Ghana

Jonas Yomboi St. John's Integrated SHTS, Navrongo, Ghana

Joana Akweley Zanu Department of Graphic Communication Design Technology, Tamale Technical University, Tamale, Ghana

Mohammed Abdul-Basit Fuseini Marketing Department, Tamale Technical University, Tamale, Ghana

Musah Bukari Department of Graphic Communication Design Technology, Tamale Technical University, Tamale, Ghana

Mohammed Majeed Department of Marketing, Tamale Technical University, Tamale, Ghana

Parag Shukla Department of Commerce and Business Management, The Maharaja Sayajirao University of Baroda, Gujarat, India

Salifu Shani Chicago School of Professional Psychology, Chicago, United State

Sofia Devi Shamurailatpam Department of Banking and Insurance, The Maharaja Sayajirao University of Baroda, Gujarat, India

Seidu Alhassan Secretaryship and Management Department, Tamale Technical University, Tamale, Ghana

Sulemana Ibrahim Department of Marketing, Tamale Technical University, Tamale, Ghana

S. Jayadatta KLE's Institute of Management Studies and Research (IMSR), Karnataka, India

Sulemana Anas Department of Marketing, Tamale Technical University, Tamale, Ghana

Vijaya Kittu Manda PBMEIT, Visakhapatnam, Andhra Pradesh, India

CHAPTER 1

Internet of Things in Marketing: An Introduction

Mohammed Majeed[1,*], **Vijaya Kittu Manda**[2], **Sulemana Ibrahim**[1] and **Esther Asiedu**[3]

[1] *Department of Marketing, Tamale Technical University, Tamale, Ghana*

[2] *PBMEIT, Visakhapatnam, Andhra Pradesh, India*

[3] *Ghana Communication Technology University, Accra, Ghana*

Abstract: The Internet of Things (IoT) has evolved into a worldwide infrastructure that facilitates advanced services through the interconnection of diverse entities, both tangible and intangible, utilizing information system technology. This study is an analysis of the impact of Internet of Things (IoT) technology on business and marketing. The study provides a comprehensive examination of IoT technology, encompassing important aspects, operational domains, and many applications within the realms of business and marketing. Companies globally are increasingly directing their attention towards the Internet of Things (IoT) due to its capacity to provide remarkable growth prospects rather than being influenced just by the prevailing buzz surrounding it. This chapter presents an introductory overview of the impact of the Internet of Things (IoT) on marketing and business domains.

Keywords: Internet of things, Technologies, Marketing, Organizations.

INTRODUCTION

Numerous firms are currently engaged in the development of technologies that possess the capability to autonomously interact with customer support systems and promptly deliver feedback to clients. According to Britt (2021), the integration of the Internet of Things (IoT) is causing significant changes in the realm of business, particularly in the domains of production and product creation. With the assistance of the ongoing epidemic, firms are currently able to enhance and ensure improved customer experiences that prioritize safety. The Internet of Things (IoT) technology is being utilized on a global scale, finding applications in various sectors like product flow monitoring, supply chain management, building automation, healthcare systems, and security infrastructure (Sharma & Gupta, 2021). In addition to product quality, clients in the tourism and hospitality

* **Corresponding author Mohammed Majeed:** Department of Marketing, Tamale Technical University, Tamale, Ghana; E-mail: tunteya14june@gmail.com

Mohammed Majeed, Jonas Yomboi, Sulemana Ibrahim & Esther Asiedu (Eds.)

industry also prioritize the technology employed in their experiences. From the standpoint of IoT customers, several key aspects come into consideration, including security, the provision of smart services encompassing various domains such as homes, buildings, cities, health, transportation, and industry, and the impact on healthcare and the potential for innovation (Lee, 2019). The Internet of Things (IoT) has been successfully used across various industries, including cities, hospitality, tourism, healthcare, and transportation. The tourism and hospitality industry is characterized by its interconnectedness with many sectors, owing to its wide range of activities encompassing various services, including transportation and museums (Li, 2021). According to Sharma and Gupta (2021), the Internet of Things (IoT) has the potential to make significant contributions to the field of tourism, particularly in the areas of personalization and enhancing the overall tourist experience. The concept of the Internet of Things (IoT) pertains to the interconnection of things and systems, establishing a networked relationship between these entities and human users. This chapter presents the concept of the Internet of Things (IoT) and connected things as a progressive advancement in technological development. According to Batat (2022), this technology has the capability to convert both basic and intricate everyday items into interconnected objects, enabling a comprehensive understanding of consumers and facilitating the provision of personalized and seamless customer experiences across online and offline channels. These technologies facilitate the implementation of applications and services across various domains, including but not limited to medicine, wellness, home automation, agriculture, the manufacturing sector, transport, logistics, and ready-to-wear. The initial section of this chapter examines the relationship between interconnected devices and the Internet of Things (IoT). Subsequently, an examination of the effects of these technologies on customer experience and consumer behavior is provided. According to Ivanov *et al.* (2017), subsequent to this, firms have the potential to revolutionize their interactions with customers through the utilization of the Internet of Things (IoT) and connected objects. This presents many prospects, advantages, and obstacles.

The integration of Internet of Things (IoT) technology in the realms of business and marketing is of utmost importance, encompassing both the operational and customer-facing aspects. This integration facilitates the development of intelligent goods and the implementation of targeted marketing campaigns to engage with customers effectively. The provision of IoT support by companies has the potential to generate value, facilitate strategic decision-making, foster innovation, enhance design processes, and ensure the security of customer service. In the context of consumer behavior, it is noteworthy that the Internet of Things (IoT) exerts a significant impact on individuals' inclinations to acquire products. The current body of research concerning the impact of the Internet of Things (IoT) on business and marketing is still relatively limited. However, this presents promising prospects for future studies, particularly in investigating the interplay between IoT and business model innovation, framework development, dark side behavior, demand service, customer preference, marketer behavior, adoption of new-age technology, conceptual understanding, network dynamics, and big data analysis. The Internet of Things (IoT) technology facilitates the integration of individuals, processes, data, and other objects into a cohesive network, resulting in the generation of valuable insights that can be translated into tangible actions. This capability has the potential to generate novel experiences and possibilities for entrepreneurs and business professionals (Ivanov *et al.*, 2017). The current potential presented by technology is unparalleled since it allows for engagement with a staggering number of 4.5 billion internet users. The aforementioned circumstances offer many opportunities for enterprises to devise novel business strategies in order to expand their market presence (Lee, 2019). This chapter presents an introductory overview of the impact of the Internet of Things (IoT) on marketing and business domains.

This chapter aims to address a research gap in the existing literature by providing a comprehensive analysis of the relationship between the Internet of Things (IoT) and critical domains within the realms of business and marketing. Furthermore, this chapter elucidates how the amalgamation of these factors might foster the formulation of more robust marketing tactics, along with its ramifications on the realm of the company. The findings of this chapter indicate the necessity for future research endeavors that are more extensive and thorough in order to go deeper into the subject matter and examine the rate at which technology is advancing.

LITERATURE

Internet of Things (IoTs)

The inception of the Internet of Things (IoT) was first documented in 1999, as noted by Marek and Woźniczka (2017). The technology in question has significantly contributed to the development of a communication framework that facilitates connectivity between diverse devices. This has resulted in the establishment of methods of communication that are not just between individuals but also amongst organizations and multiple systems (Abdel-Basset *et al.*, 2019). Furthermore, it enables the acquisition of data from several devices and facilitates their storage. The Internet of Things (IoT) significantly contributes to enhancing operational efficiency as a result of its exceptional capacity to gather extensive amounts of data (Song & Li, 2020). The Internet is a significant innovation that is extensively utilized by individuals across diverse businesses (Nasereddin & Faqir, 2019). The primary aim of this initiative is to disseminate knowledge and enhance global communication across diverse disciplines (Nasereddin & Faqir, 2019). The phrase "Internet of Things" serves as a comprehensive term that includes all applications pertaining to the expansion of the Internet and the web into the realm of tangible entities. The extension is achieved by employing spatially distributed devices that possess embedded identification, sensing, and actuation capabilities (Miorandi *et al.*, 2012). In more accessible terms, the Internet of Things (IoT) refers to a worldwide network of interconnected machines and gadgets that have the ability to communicate and interact with one another through web applications (Marek & Woźniczka, 2017). The network's interconnected items not only gather data from their surroundings but also utilize established internet protocols to offer services for information transmission, analysis, applications, and communication.

Internet of Things in Marketing

The focus of this chapter is to review literature on the different uses of the Internet of Things (IoT) within the field of marketing. Specifically, it examines how IoT can be utilized to customize content and establish a data-driven marketing framework. These applications enable marketers to create distinct experiences that bridge the gap between the digital and physical realms, foster stronger connections with consumers, and deliver highly contextual and personalized messages. This comprehensive reference book encompasses essential subjects, including corporate image, social networking sites, and website building. It is particularly well-suited for individuals involved in business ownership, management, marketing, research, academia, professional practice, teaching, and learning. The Internet of Things (IoT) not only retrieves publicly shared information from platforms such as social media but also gathers data pertaining to individuals' daily routines and activities. The range of IoT-enabled gadgets that will be employed by the average consumer encompasses various categories, including coffee makers, thermostats, home automation systems, and wearable devices such as smartwatches. These devices play a crucial role in the daily lives of consumers, encompassing activities from waking up in the morning to going to bed at night. The availability of lifestyle trend data empowers digital marketers to gain insights into the utilization patterns of specific products or services, including the timing, frequency, and motivations behind their usage. Experiential marketing has contributed to a more pragmatic and hands-on approach to the concept of experience, with a focus on creating meaningful and memorable experiences for consumers. This approach involves engaging consumers in direct interaction with the firm and its offerings from the standpoint of experience marketing, according to Batat (2019a). In the context of the increasing commoditization of goods and services, the significance of customer experiences has emerged as a pivotal factor for enterprises in maintaining a competitive edge. An experience is manifested when a corporation deliberately employs services as the platform and goods as the supporting elements and actively involves clients in a manner that generates a noteworthy occurrence. Commodities possess the quality of fungibility, goods exhibit tangibility, services demonstrate intangibility, and experiences elicit memorability. Furthermore, Moradi and Badrinarayanan (2021) demonstrate that marketing and communication actions play a significant role in shaping consuming experiences. These experiences are influenced by the strategies and programs undertaken by enterprises to develop captivating experiential products, hence captivating and delighting their customers. Within this context, it is evident that there exist four prominent marketing and communication methods that are specifically designed to foster the creation of immersive experiences. These strategies include consumer engagement, theming, narrative, and sensory marketing. Consumer engagement involves a substantial human element that pertains to the relationship between the consumer and the organization. The establishment and development of this connection can occur and progress throughout the entirety of the customer's experience, whether it is in a physical location or a digital environment.

The integration of the Internet of Things (IoT) and social media platforms has the potential to significantly enhance marketing channels and tools. Currently, organizations are utilizing social media platforms as a means to gather feedback pertaining to their products and services (Ray, 2018). According to Caro and Sadr (2019), the convergence of Internet of Things (IoT) technologies with social media platforms has the potential to create a digital environment that facilitates a more intimate relationship between a firm and its target audience. Furthermore, the potential for expanding the client base is heightened when personal data is shared (Vermesan & Friess, 2014). In general, it is anticipated that IoT technologies may assume a crucial role within the framework of integrated marketing communications (IMC) and bring about a fundamental restructuring of commercial communication systems.

The attainment of profitability in various businesses is contingent upon customer happiness, as it facilitates the reduction of operational expenses and the augmentation of profits (Choi, 2019). Customer satisfaction is the ultimate outcome of assessment protocols. The feedback of customer evaluation of the service supplied is ultimately determined by the psychological satisfaction derived from meeting consumer expectations (Faqir, 2019). According to Mostafa *et al.* (2019), when customers' initial expectations are fulfilled or surpassed, they are more likely to experience a sense of satisfaction. In order to maintain client satisfaction and happiness, a significant number of firms endeavor to comprehend the needs and desires of their customers (Nasereddin & Faqir, 2019). Marketers have the ability to utilize customer behavior data in order to enhance customer experiences and optimize the arrangement and presentation of products, particularly within a retail setting. The objective of achieving real-time engagement may be significant, but it is crucial to emphasize that real-time optimization, extending beyond the confines of message context, holds even greater significance, particularly in domains beyond the narrow scope of marketing. The attainment of customer satisfaction extends beyond the mere process of purchasing and resolving concerns. The establishment of trust in data utilization is crucial for harnessing the full potential of the Internet of Things (IoT) in marketing. The true efficacy of IoT in marketing rests in marketers' capacity to think innovatively and enhance customer experiences on a larger scale, irrespective of touch points or phases within the customer life cycle.

The Internet of Things (IoT) has emerged as a pivotal tool for augmenting various facets of marketing research. According to Pauget and Dammak (2019), the utilization of Internet of Things (IoT) technology can provide marketing managers with enhanced technical capabilities, enabling them to effectively strategize and execute comprehensive marketing research initiatives. To ensure the successful completion of this research, it is important to take into account a multitude of aspects (Ray, 2018). One example of the utilization of convenience as a strategic marketing tactic is its role as a prominent characteristic of customer experience and overall brand perception. By leveraging IoT platforms for marketing research, marketing managers are able to develop a positive rapport with consumers through effective approaches and communication strategies. According to Allhoff and Henschke (2018), the incorporation of Internet of Things (IoT) capabilities, including Machine-to-Machine (M2M) communication, automation, and big data, can effectively expedite the process of marketing managers in recognizing potential marketing prospects and accurately dividing the marketplace into distinct segments. The Internet of Things (IoT) has made significant advancements in the field of marketing automation. Traditionally, the process of manually gathering and collecting data requires substantial time and patience. However, the integration of IoT has revolutionized data management, making it a more efficient and streamlined task. Moreover, the data presented offers both the necessary and sufficient information required to effectively execute automated programs, hence minimizing the workload for marketers. In former generations, marketers were burdened with the arduous task of independently collecting, compiling, and constructing databases. However, they have now been relieved of these excessive duties. The contemporary landscape of marketing has seen significant transformations in comparison to previous decades. It may be argued that the emergence of the Internet of Things (IoT) has fundamentally altered the role and understanding of marketers, providing a novel interpretation of this professional designation (Tudor *et al.*, 2021). Hence, the interaction between the consumer and the organization holds significant importance. The successful execution of a comprehensive and inclusive marketing strategy poses a significant obstacle for organizations seeking to both acquire and retain customers, all the while distinguishing themselves within a fiercely competitive market. The current difficult circumstances push organizations to transition their emphasis from a conventional marketing method to a more experienced marketing approach that prioritizes the client and their discernible and imperceptible requirements (Moradi *et al.*, 2017). The utilization of the Internet of Things (IoT) in operational contexts yields customer-centric data that can effectively contribute to providing product assistance for consumers of smart devices. The organization has the capacity to offer both requested and unsolicited advice or recommendations to consumers regarding the optimal utilization of the refrigerator, with a focus on the energy economy. Furthermore, the company can offer assistance to customers regarding the optimal temperature for preserving stored products in the refrigerator for extended periods of time, leveraging the wealth of detailed information accessible *via* the Internet (Tariq *et al.*, 2020). Furthermore, in the event that the contents kept within the refrigerator exceed its designated capacity, it might potentially impact the overall functionality of the appliance. In such cases, the company has the ability to provide guidance and notifications to the customer regarding this matter. In addition, users have the option to seek assistance from the company (Tariq *et al.*, 2020) for guidance pertaining to the installation or functionality of any feature. The provision of product assistance, whether solicited or unsolicited, is expected to enhance the overall customer experience and increase customer satisfaction levels. According to Pauget and Dammak (2019), the Internet of Things (IoTs) has the potential to serve as a basis for customer-centric marketing. The utilization of Internet of Things (IoT) devices has been observed to mitigate the inconvenience associated with the advertisement process. This is due to the inherent flexibility offered by these technologies, allowing the target audience to conveniently access product or brand-related information according to their individual preferences and choices (Moradi & Badrinarayanan, 2021).

There is a growing trend among consumers to exhibit an increasing inclination toward embracing mobile and wearable applications during the purchasing process. The phenomenon described is of great interest to businesses, as it enables them to gather data on consumer behavior, including purchasing habits and demographic characteristics such as age, gender, and social position (Madakam *et al.*, 2015). This will additionally assist firms in cultivating qualitative and quantitative databases that have the potential to enhance the processes of product development, supply chain management, advertising tactics, and marketing research. It is imperative for organizations to prioritize the potential of IoT platforms in order to actively pursue customer insights that are based on location. Market segmentation is a fundamental element of marketing research, encompassing several components such as market intelligence, industry trends, data analysis, SWOT analysis, and PEST analysis (Pauget & Dammak, 2019).

The utilization of the Internet of Things (IoT) allows marketers to provide personalized and contextually relevant messages to consumers. This is exemplified by the integration of digital billboards in physical environments, where smartphones or other digital devices facilitate interactive engagements. In the retail sector, marketers are progressively turning their attention toward the Internet of Things (IoT) within the purchasing environment.

The data accessible *via* these Internet of Things (IoT) goods encompasses a variety of information, such as customer profiles that include demographic and geographic details, consumer preferences, utility patterns, product usage timing, and frequency of use categorized as heavy or light. Therefore, the data may possess either organized or unstructured characteristics, and its extensive magnitude presents challenges in comprehending and interpreting it (Tariq *et al.*, 2020). Furthermore, the data exhibits real-time characteristics and possesses inherent uncertainty in capturing past trends. Consequently, it is deemed unsuitable for immediate analysis and necessitates storage and subsequent examination after a designated period of time. Nevertheless, if the data is preserved and managed in an appropriate manner, there is a possibility that it can serve as a viable alternative to customer market research surveys, offering cost-effectiveness. Upon recognizing the significance of customer-driven data obtained from Internet of Things (IoT) devices, corporations might proceed to analyze said data in order to derive marketing consequences. Marketing encompasses a broader scope than solely the data-driven marketing context associated with the Internet of Things. The Internet of Things (IoT) empowers marketers to cultivate distinct encounters that connect the digital and physical realms. This is particularly evident when they venture beyond conventional tailored messages and explore innovative approaches. Currently, the majority of Internet of Things (IoT) initiatives primarily focus on enhancing efficiency and streamlining operations, with objectives that have limited direct impact on consumer satisfaction and engagement.

BENEFITS OF IOT IN MARKETING

Targeted Advertising

The practice of targeted advertising refers to the strategic approach employed by marketers to deliver personalized advertisements to certain individuals or groups based on their demographic. By gathering data on user activity, the Internet of Things (IoT) has the potential to develop more intelligent and efficient campaigns that are customized to users' preferences, hence increasing the likelihood of user engagement. An illustrative use is the implementation of iBeacons by Apple, enabling retail establishments to track client entrances and deliver tailored promotional offers to adjacent individuals through their iPhones. The utilization of compact sensors that are linked to the store's WiFi network enables the precise determination of a phone's location, hence facilitating the delivery of personalized notifications to nearby devices. This technology has the potential to inform clients about discounts that are tailored to their previous shopping patterns or preferences. Through the use of personalized strategies, organizations may effectively engage in product promotion while simultaneously catering to the desires and preferences of their target consumers.

Added Value and Competitive Advantage

The concept of competitive advantages refers to the unique attributes or capabilities possessed by a company that set it apart from its competitors and enable it to outperform them in the marketplace. These advantages can take several forms, such as superior product quality and lower production costs. The Internet of Things (IoT) encompasses novel attributes and offerings that enhance the worth of enterprises, facilitating their ability to distinguish themselves from rivals. An illustration of the potential benefits of employing sensors to optimize land utilization, irrigation practices, and fertilizer application is the production of agricultural goods that exhibit enhanced freshness and environmental sustainability (Ulloa, 2019).

Facilitated Innovation

In the realm of marketing, innovation stands out as a highly attractive avenue for using the potential of the Internet of Things (IoT). As an illustration, an automotive dealership has the capacity to integrate Internet of Things (IoT)-enabled displays within their showroom, thereby enabling consumers to promptly choose the desired specifications for their ideal vehicle and observe a live visual representation of it. Customers are now unrestricted by the availability of vehicles in physical inventory. Alternatively, individuals now have the ability to design and personalize vehicles according to their specific preferences and financial constraints.

The Optimization of Processes and Operations for Enhanced Efficiency

The availability of real-time data regarding the state of products and/or services enables the opportunity to enhance operational procedures and enhance overall productivity (Merenych, 2023). An illustration of the potential benefits of the Internet of Things (IoT) may be observed in the accurate calculation of the shipping duration for a consignment of flowers from Colombia to Europe. This precise calculation enables the flowers to reach their destination in optimal condition, thereby significantly reducing wastage (Ulloa, 2019).

The IoTs Aids Equipment Maintenance Needs

Factories allocate substantial financial resources towards the repair and maintenance of their equipment. Furthermore, each interruption in production results in a substantial financial setback. This could potentially lead to injuries among plant workers. Nevertheless, interconnected sensors possess the capability to consistently assess the operational efficiency of machinery, hence enabling the timely identification of any alterations prior to a potential failure. According to Merenych (2023), in the event that a flaw is identified in the tool, the system possesses the capability to autonomously arrange maintenance activities to rectify the issue prior to it escalating into a significant concern.

The Act of Disrupting Business Models

This phenomenon facilitates the emergence of novel business models and consumer paradigms, such as the sharing economy or pay-per-use, which engage several stakeholders in a synchronized fashion. One illustration can be observed in the context of a hotel wherein the coordination of its availability and menus is entirely autonomous, aligning seamlessly with the scheduled arrival of tourism buses (Ulloa, 2019). IoT also helps *in s*upporting business models with empirical evidence. The utilization of data is increasingly becoming recognized as a potent tool across several industries. In the context of the automobile sector, there is a growing trend towards the use of Internet of Things (IoT) technology. This adoption aims to facilitate the seamless collection and tracking of data by vehicles, enabling them to effectively engage with smart city solutions. Through these endeavors, the automotive industry is undergoing a significant transformation towards data-driven business models.

Monitoring

The act of monitoring refers to the systematic observation and assessment of a particular situation or process. Internet of Things (IoT) devices facilitate the provision of advanced inventory monitoring capabilities and location tracking for organizations, resulting in heightened efficiency in storage and distribution processes. Companies have the capability to determine the locations where goods have delays during the shipping process. According to Merenych (2023), supply chain managers can enhance their route planning capabilities by leveraging IoT data analytics, which enables them to consider various factors such as weather dangers, accidents, and road conditions.

Digitalized Factory

A factory that utilizes extensive equipment connectivity has exceptional performance in comparison to traditional factories. According to Merenych (2023), substantial outcomes can be achieved through the implementation of remote management, automation of operations, and optimization strategies. The installation of inventory management systems is further facilitated by the increased efficiency of these factories. In an organization where the majority of operations are automated and dependent on bespoke software, the occurrence of human mistakes is significantly minimized. Moreover, many repetitive tasks might be delegated to automated devices, which have the capability to operate continuously without interruption. According to Merenych (2023), this phenomenon is characterized by increased levels of working productivity coupled with reduced expenses.

Enhance Prospects for Corporate Growth and Financial Gain

The Internet of Things (IoT) presents a multitude of possibilities for the emergence of novel business models and avenues for generating revenue. It facilitates organizations in leveraging contemporary business concepts and solutions. The implementation of Internet of Things (IoT) technology facilitates the advancement of various industries by enabling the development of robust applications, reducing the time required to bring products to market, and enhancing the financial gains achieved from investments. The Internet of Things (IoT) possesses the potential to revolutionize the manner in which businesses engage with the global audience by expanding the reach of IoT and further enhancing connectivity to provide consumers with the advantages associated with IoT.

Intelligent Security Systems

Contemporary security systems encompass functionalities beyond just surveillance, enabling users to monitor many locations remotely, including multiple offices or storage areas. By leveraging artificial intelligence, smart cameras possess the capability to identify and discern facial features, hence enabling the detection of unfamiliar individuals who may have gained unauthorized entry into a restricted area. According to Merenych (2023), the use of sensors equipped with noise or movement recognition capabilities contributes to the prevention of robberies and enhances the overall safety of production facilities.

Delivery Tracking

The ability to monitor the progress of one's orders is particularly advantageous when it comes to global or intercontinental shipments. Compact sensors have the capability to transmit signals pertaining to the precise whereabouts of commodities and provide an estimation of the anticipated time of arrival. In addition, it is possible for them to provide reports regarding the condition of delivery, encompassing factors such as the weather, humidity, and shaking level. This capability is particularly advantageous in the context of managing perishable commodities (Merenych, 2023).

A Deeper Understanding of Consumer Behavior

Enhanced availability of information and data facilitates a more profound comprehension of client preferences, precisely timed throughout the manufacturing process or the supervision of the product (Ulloa, 2019).

Enhancement of Customer Service and Insight (Experience)

Ensuring the prosperity of a firm is contingent upon the provision of high-quality customer service. Cutting-edge Internet of Things (IoT) technology, such as intelligent trackers and portable card readers, are employed to augment client experiences. Mobile card readers have the capability to establish a connection with smartphones, facilitating seamless transaction processing. Additionally, the utilization of smart trackers empowers consumers to effectively monitor their items, hence enhancing overall satisfaction levels. Currently, numerous corporate organizations employ hyper-local advertising and couponing strategies in conjunction with IoT technology to enhance client satisfaction and fulfill their specific target objectives. Utility service providers have the capability to leverage IoT solutions for the purpose of identifying and resolving issues through the utilization of smart meters and other smart grid technology.

Enhance Business Operations and Promote Workplace Safety

There is a growing endeavor to develop IoT solutions with high levels of security, as this has emerged as a critical milestone in the transformation of many enterprises. Industry experts are currently prioritizing the management of critical security risks associated with business solutions related to the Internet of Things (IoT) in order to enhance the extensive adoption of this technological advancement. Internet of Things (IoT) devices have the potential to enable organizations to enhance labor safety and bolster workplace security. The implementation of embedded wearables and sensors enables continuous monitoring and hazard notification for employees operating in high-risk environments such as heavy industries, mining, and real estate or construction sectors. Small and medium-sized enterprises (SMEs) have the ability to employ connected video surveillance cameras and smart locks in order to continuously monitor their office premises and ensure the protection of valuable assets.

Enhance Levels of Production and Augment Competence

Enhancing productivity and competence is a primary strategy that firms can employ to ensure profitability. Internet of Things (IoT) devices have the potential to provide valuable support to manufacturing industries by facilitating accurate demand assessment and efficient management of various production stages. This is achieved through the capability of IoT devices to provide real-time tracking of equipment parts and on-hand raw materials. However, it is worth noting that firms have the ability to collect worker data in order to assess their periods of high productivity, which can then be used to effectively schedule important activities and meetings. Smart devices can be enhanced through the implementation of the Internet of Things (IoT) in organizational settings, which involves educating staff members about potential technical issues and establishing prearranged remote troubleshooting protocols. They have the capability to facilitate and streamline daily operational chores, such as programming tea or coffee machines to operate on predetermined schedules, hence enhancing the efficiency of organizational processes.

Assistance is Requested in Conducting an Analysis of Consumer Behavior

The examination of customer preferences and behavior holds great importance in ensuring the success of many industries and businesses. The implementation of the Internet of Things (IoT) in retail enterprises enables them to acquire, monitor, and analyze data collected from many sources, such as the Internet, video surveillance, social media, and mobile usage, hence providing several advantages. This scenario provides valuable information for predicting consumer preferences and future business trends, enabling organizations to effectively build goods and deliver customized services to enhance customer engagement. By gaining access to comprehensive client profiles, organizations will have the ability to retain their desired consumer base and foster brand loyalty.

Reducing Operational Expenses

The incorporation of Internet of Things (IoT) technologies offers firms additional benefits, such as cost reduction and improved sustainability in their business operations. These possibilities can be realized when firms establish a continuous connection with a large number of smart devices over the Internet, enabling the Internet of Things (IoT) to support businesses in making more intelligent decisions based on real-time operational insights while simultaneously reducing associated running costs. IoT devices have the potential to enhance operational efficiency in manufacturing businesses through equipment tracking and proactive identification of potential problems or errors on the production line, hence minimizing downtime. Business enterprises have the potential to reduce their overall energy costs and enhance electrical efficiency through the adoption and implementation of Internet of Things (IoT) solutions. Furthermore, intelligent building systems include the capability to monitor, track, and control excessive utilization of electrical systems.

Enhancing the Capabilities of Intelligent Device Applications

Smart devices have become increasingly prevalent across various industries. The proliferation of smart device applications is expected to continue expanding across several business domains, facilitated by the Internet of Things (IoT). These sectors encompass healthcare, transportation, entertainment, hospitality, and education.

IoT in the Near Future

IoT technologies are poised to have significant and enduring effects across various industries in the foreseeable future. By employing vigilant methods and strategic approaches, the implementation of Internet of Things (IoT) technologies has the potential to enhance profitability and yield various advantages for enterprises. The Internet of Things (IoT) has emerged as a highly sought-after technology, surpassing other new technologies in terms of consumer interest and aspirations. Despite the potential value that the Internet of Things (IoT) can offer, enterprises must overcome significant hurdles, such as those related to knowledge and data administration, the absence of interconnected technology, and concerns around privacy. The Internet of Things (IoT) is a transformative technology that is currently exerting a significant impact on several facets of company operations, encompassing manufacturing, distribution, marketing, and servicing clients. The advent of Internet of Things (IoT) devices holds the promise of enhancing our quality of life and concurrently presents numerous avenues for company growth and development. However, there exist substantial obstacles that must be addressed in order to fully capitalize on these prospects. An escalation in competition is anticipated by prominent industry leaders, namely Microsoft and Google. The prevalence of extensive Internet of Things (IoT) systems will likely result in their market dominance. These significant players are expected to acquire a substantial share of the market and continue to expand their organizational groups in order to scale the associated technologies. As the competition for market dominance intensifies among full-scale IoT platforms, it is anticipated that smaller and medium-sized firms will strategically focus on specialized niche markets and specific industry segments in order to ensure their subsistence.

Implication

The significance of the Internet of Things (IoT) in enhancing decision-making processes within the field of marketing research is of paramount importance. The implementation of Internet of Things (IoT) technologies holds the capacity to revolutionize the field of marketing research. It is imperative to augment folks' comprehension of the ways in which Internet of Things (IoT) tools might be leveraged to their benefit. The automated generation of real-time data streams facilitates marketing researchers in discerning efficacious ways for fostering favorable client engagement. The increased availability of consumer data enhances the decision-making capabilities of both academics and practitioners, as it enables them to make more informed and confident decisions. The deployment of Internet of Things (IoT) solutions presents a wide array of opportunities for augmenting marketing research. This is particularly true for digital marketers who want access to extensive data regarding consumer trends and opinions related to the continuous utilization of Internet of Things (IoT) technologies. The availability of a larger volume of data for analysis is perceived as beneficial for digital marketers, as it provides them with the possibility to optimize particular procedures and effectively engage with various target consumer segments. The clear prospect of doing predictive analysis on the needs and preferences of target customers arises from the direct linkage between the Internet of Things (IoT) and cloud computing. IoT-enabled items have the potential to influence consumer product usage patterns by establishing a connection between the benefits derived from the product and its actual usage. For example, by utilizing the mobile application, the manufacturer has the capability to monitor whether the user is consistently adhering to the recommended maintenance practices outlined in the product documentation. The cultivation of positive behavior can be effectively promoted by associating it with non-monetary incentives. This approach not only leads to customer satisfaction but also fosters stronger connections between the firm and its clientele. In conclusion, the integration of IoT technology into products can effectively diminish consumer bargaining power through the amplification of economic switching costs for enterprises. The potential loss of customer data stored on the Internet of Things (IoT) device embedded in the refrigerator may influence the consumer's preference for the manufacturer's product over that of a competitor, as switching to a different brand could result in the loss of said data. Increased duration and greater engagement with the product will enhance customer retention, driven by concerns around the potential loss of user-centric longitudinal data. The Internet of Things (IoT) will play a significant role in formulating a customer relationship management (CRM) strategy for manufacturers. As an expert in the field of digital marketing, it is imperative that you prioritize the protection of customer privacy, particularly in light of the anticipated spike in consumer data in the coming era. While there is a favorable response from a significant number of consumers towards personalized product offerings and sales funnels that cater to their individual preferences and requirements, there is also a concurrent emphasis on the need for privacy, both in the online and offline realms. One significant obstacle that the digital marketing business must address is the development of individualized purchasing experiences while avoiding the perception of intrusiveness. In order to synchronize digital marketing tactics with customer expectations, it is imperative to exhibit a heightened level of security and guarantee the protection of consumer information during the analysis process

The evolution of technology usage will necessitate a corresponding transformation in data collection methods, prompting marketers to adapt their strategies for leveraging this data and engaging with customers. It is crucial for digital marketers to commence their preparations in anticipation of the significant transformations that will inevitably be introduced by the Internet of Things (IoT). Begin by establishing a foundation of trust and empathy towards the intended recipients of your message, and cultivate a genuine rapport with their desires and anticipations commencing at present. Ensure that your business is in sync with your target audience and capitalize on the Internet of Things (IoT) advancements to enhance and optimize your digital marketing approach. To effectively progress in the realm of IoT technologies, solutions, and services, it is advisable to engage the services of a skilled IoT service provider. The contracted company has the capacity to facilitate the utilization of Internet of Things (IoT) services, so allowing for the realization of associated advantages and the mitigation of associated obstacles. Consequently, this can result in an enhancement of the return on investment.

CONCLUSION

In light of the increasing interconnectedness of modern society and the rapid speed of technological advancements, the Internet of Things (IoT) has become increasingly prevalent and accessible. Consequently, businesses are compelled to embrace IoT solutions in order to enhance the experiences of their clientele. The Internet of Things (IoT) facilitates the interconnection and data exchange between physical devices over the Internet, allowing for the collection of strategic information. This capability presents enterprises with the potential to enhance their operational efficiency and responsiveness to market dynamics. The advent of IoT solutions has presented marketers with novel capabilities to transform conventional marketing practices by substituting them with more comprehensive and precise types of data analysis. The utilization of Internet of Things (IoT) devices has been demonstrated to have a positive impact on the augmentation of information interchange in the domains of marketing and research. The advent of Internet of Things (IoT) technology has provided digital marketing experts with a diverse array of tools and tactics, allowing them to enhance their research methods and introduce novel perspectives to the field of marketing. In conclusion, the utilization of the Internet of Things (IoT) in the field of marketing entails adopting innovative approaches and providing pertinent services that hold significant value for customers in their everyday lives.

In summary, the Internet of Things (IoT) is fundamentally transforming the landscape of our digitally oriented marketing industry. The adoption of this state-of-the-art technology provides firms with a means to enhance their performance and remain abreast of contemporary trends. In order to achieve optimal outcomes, it is imperative for organizations to allocate resources toward appropriate software solutions, formulate robust plans, give precedence to the demands of customers, and demonstrate a willingness to engage in ongoing testing and experimentation. Furthermore, there exist a multitude of distinctive enterprises that act as trailblazers in employing various applications of the Internet of Things (IoT), serving as a source of inspiration for other corporations seeking to capitalize on this cutting-edge technological trend. It is imperative not to underestimate or dismiss the significance of this resource. Instead, one should take advantage of its potential and carefully analyze the multitude of advantages it offers over an extended period.

REFERENCES

Abdel-Basset, M., Mohamed, M., Chang, V., Smarandache, F. (2019). IoT and its impact on the electronics market: A powerful decision support system for helping customers in choosing the best product. *Symmetry,* *11*(5), 611.
[http://dx.doi.org/10.3390/sym11050611]

Batat, W. (2019). Experiential marketing: Consumer behavior, customer experience and the 7Es. Routledge.
[http://dx.doi.org/10.4324/9781315232201]

Batat, W. (2022). Chapter 6: Phygital customer experience strategy enabled by the Internet of Things (IoT) and connected objects. 130–146.
[http://dx.doi.org/10.4337/9781800371897.00016]

Choi, D-H. (2019). Impact of Internet of Things (IoT)'s Service Quality on the Hotel Customer Satisfaction. *International Journal of Recent Technology and Engineering (IJRTE)*, *8*(2S6), 362-366.
[http://dx.doi.org/10.35940/ijrte.B1069.0782S619]

Faqir.M.J.M. (2019). The Impact of Internet of Things on Customer Satisfaction: Field Study on Passengers in Queen Alia International Airport. Master dissertation. Middle East University.

Ivanov, S. (2019). Ultimate transformation: How will automation technologies disrupt the travel, tourism and hospitality industries? *Z. Tourwiss., 11*(1), 25-43.
[http://dx.doi.org/10.1515/tw-2019-0003]

Ivanov, S.H., Webster, C., Berezina, K. (2017). Adoption of robots and service automation by tourism and hospitality companies. *Rev. Tur. Desenvolv. (Aveiro),* *27*(28), 1501-1517.

Lee, I. (2019). The Internet of Things for enterprises: An ecosystem, architecture, and IoT service business model. *Internet of Things,* *7*, 100078.
[http://dx.doi.org/10.1016/j.iot.2019.100078]

Madakam, S., Ramaswamy, R., Tripathi, S. (2015). Internet of Things (IoT): A Literature Review. *Journal of Computer and Communications,* *3*(5), 164-173.
[http://dx.doi.org/10.4236/jcc.2015.35021]

Marek, L., Woźniczka, J. (2017). The Internet of Things as a customer experience tool. *Jagiellonian Journal of Management,* *3*(3), 163-176.
[http://dx.doi.org/10.4467/2450114XJJM.17.011.9562]

Merenych, S. (January 10, 2023). IoT in Business in 2023: Benefits of Implementing Internet of Things. Available from: https://clockwise.software/blog/iot-in-business-benefits-of-internet-of-things/.

Miorandi, D., Sicari, S., De Pellegrini, F., Chlamtac, I. (2012). Internet of things: Vision, applications and research challenges. *Ad Hoc Netw.,* *10*(7), 1497-1516.
[http://dx.doi.org/10.1016/j.adhoc.2012.02.016]

Moradi, M., Badrinarayanan, V. (2021). The effects of brand prominence and narrative features on crowdfunding success for entrepreneurial aftermarket enterprises. *J. Bus. Res.,* *124*, 286-298.
[http://dx.doi.org/10.1016/j.jbusres.2020.12.002]

Moradi, M., Dass, M., Pedada, K. (2017). An investigation into the role of brand affiliation and content emotions on crowdfunding success. *Creating Marketing Magic and Innovative Future Marketing Trends.* (pp. 611-615). Cham: Springer.
[http://dx.doi.org/10.1007/978-3-319-45596-9_116]

Mostafa, N., Hamdy, W., Alawady, H. (2019). Impacts of internet of things on supply chains: a framework for warehousing. Social sciences, 8(3), Nasereddin, H. H., & Faqir, M. (2019). The impact of internet of things on customer service: A preliminary study. *Periodicals of Engineering and Natural Sciences,* *7*(1), 148-155.

Song, Y., Li, Y. (2020). The Establishment of the Logical Model of the Internet of Things Application System. *J. Phys. Conf. Ser.,* *1624*(2), 022006.
[http://dx.doi.org/10.1088/1742-6596/1624/2/022006]

Sharma, U., Gupta, D. (2021). Analyzing the applications of internet of things in hotel industry. *J. Phys. Conf. Ser.,* *1969*(1), 012041.
[http://dx.doi.org/10.1088/1742-6596/1969/1/012041]

Tudor, A.I.M., Chiţu, I.B., Dovleac, L., Brătucu, G. (2021). IoT Technologies as Instruments for SMEs' Innovation and Sustainable Growth. *Sustainability,* *13*(11), 6357.
[http://dx.doi.org/10.3390/su13116357]

Tariq, B., Taimoor, S., Najam, H., Law, R., Hassan, W., &; Han, H. (2020). Generating Marketing Outcomes through Internet of Things (IoT) Technologies. *Sustainability*, *12*(22), 9670.
[http://dx.doi.org/10.3390/su12229670]

Ulloa, A. (September 5, 2019). Introduction to the IoT for companies: early opportunities. Available from: https://nae.global/en/introduction-to-the-iot-for-companies-early-opportunities/.

CHAPTER 2

Product and the Internet of Things (IoT)

Jonas Yomboi[1,*], **Mohammed Majeed**[2] and **Esther Asiedu**[3]

[1] *St. John's Integrated SHTS, Navrongo, Ghana*

[2] *Department of Marketing, Tamale Technical University, Tamale, Ghana*

[3] *Ghana Communication Technology University, Accra, Ghana*

Abstract: The implementation of a marketing mix is vital in order to enhance partner satisfaction and ensure the consistent delivery of high-quality products in sufficient quantities. The tool in question is utilized to assess the degree of achievement in marketing endeavors, encompassing elements such as product. Yet less is done conceptually on how IoTs affect product management. Hence, this chapter reviews the extant literature on the aspects of the product that IoT impacts. The primary objective of IoT technologies for enterprises is to address market needs and demands while also generating demand through the provision of a distinctive and satisfactory customer experience. The benefits include customer engagement, product innovation, exposing the utilization of the product, quality control, quality of products and services, product style, the provision of after-sales service, the product line length within the realm of IoTs commerce, various stock-keeping units (SKUS), the fulfillment of customer demand, and the breadth of firms' portfolio. Consequently, it is anticipated that this technological advancement will contribute to a prosperous period for brands.

Keywords: Internet of things, Marketing, Product, Services, Technology.

INTRODUCTION

According to Liu *et al.* (2019), the marketing idea posits that the profitability of an organization is contingent upon its ability to meet the desires and requirements of its stakeholders. By generating profits, the firm can facilitate its growth and advancement, hence enhancing the level of satisfaction experienced by its stakeholders. The implementation of a marketing mix is vital in order to enhance partner satisfaction and ensure the consistent delivery of high-quality products in sufficient quantities. The tool in question is utilized to assess the degree of achievement in marketing endeavors, encompassing elements such as product, price, distribution, and promotion (Firman *et al.*, 2020). A perpetual conflict

* **Corresponding author Jonas Yomboi:** St. John's Integrated SHTS, Navrongo, Ghana;
E-mail: jonasyomboi@gmail.com

arises between the structured aspect and the imaginative aspect of the subject matter. According to Kusuma *et al.* (2020), the discipline of effectively identifying target markets and engaging in activities aimed at attracting, keeping, and expanding customer base is referred to as the science of customer relationship management. This involves the creation, delivery, and communication of exceptional customer value. Based on the findings of the literature review, it has been shown that marketing activity and innovation are the primary mechanisms *via* which value is generated for customers. Moreover, the proliferation of digital technologies has prompted numerous scholars to explore the potential of utilizing these technologies to expand marketing endeavors as a means of fostering innovation within organizations (Baumgärtner & Winkler, 2003). The Internet of Things (IoT) has emerged as a prominent and widely adopted technology within the realm of digital technologies. It has opened up new avenues for doing innovative research in the field of marketing operations. The advent of Internet of Things (IoT) applications has had a profound impact on several aspects of human existence, significantly enhancing the efficacy and significance of endeavors undertaken by individuals and organizations alike. In the present era, a vast number of commonplace items have been integrated with sophisticated sensors, wireless networks, and cutting-edge computing functionalities. The proliferation of these technologies has led to the emergence of wearables, smart home applications, sophisticated healthcare systems, "smart cities", and industrial automation (Chen & Ji, 2016; Marjani *et al.*, 2017). After a prolonged period of ambiguity, the Internet of Things (IoT) appears to be on the verge of transitioning into widespread adoption within the realm of corporate operations. There is a growing trend in the adoption of IoT technology by enterprises, as evidenced by the predicted global count of IoT-connected devices reaching 43 billion by 2023 (Gupta *et al.*, 2017). The Internet of Things (IoT) exemplifies the increasing inclination toward physical items that feature both computer and communication capabilities, enabling them to collaboratively collect information in real time (Guo *et al.*, 2013).

During the period prior to the advent of the Internet of Things (IoT), consumer items were mostly developed with the intention of possessing aesthetic appeal, ensuring user safety, exhibiting durability, offering cost-effectiveness, generating desirability, and eventually fulfilling their intended functionalities. The design of a product remains substantially unchanged from its pre-sensor, pre-processing capabilities, and pre-software integration era. However, smart products possess basic distinctions from their non-intelligent counterparts. By utilizing enhanced network flexibility, including artificial intelligence, and possessing the ability to deploy, automate, orchestrate, and protect a wide range of devices on a large scale, the Internet of Things (IoT) facilitates the connection and data exchange between billions of objects and systems (Kumar & Nayak, 2018). Currently, there is a trend in which commonplace gadgets such as dishwashers, thermostats, dryers, and refrigerators are being engineered to gather and exchange data, resulting in the establishment of an interconnected network of systems. The Internet of Things (IoT) phenomenon has been examined from both technological and conceptual perspectives. The technical components of the Internet of Things (IoT) were examined by researchers Tan and Wang (2010), who focused on topics such as interoperability, architecture, and identification. These features were also explored by Haller *et al.* (2009), who emphasized the importance of addressing and managing heterogeneity and interoperability within the IoT. In contrast, numerous scholars have undertaken theoretical investigations of the Internet of Things (IoT) with regard to various stakeholders, including users, governments, and companies (Haller *et al.*, 2009; Peoples *et al.*, 2013; Weber, 2010; Zhao *et al.*, 2013). Yet less is done conceptually on how IoT affects product management. Hence, this chapter reviews the extant literature on the aspects of the product that IoT impacts.

LITERATURE

IoT

The Internet of Things (IoT) is a term used to describe technology that connects almost all devices. These interconnected things must have addresses, distinctive identifiers, and Internet connectivity. IoT devices can include almost anything, including computers, cars, people, sensors, and refrigerators (Cuit, 2016). IoT technology makes it possible for physical objects to have virtual representations by connecting them to the internet. IoT technology has greatly benefited from contemporary advancements in communication, applications, and equipment (such as wireless sensor networks and radio frequency identification). IoT infrastructures produce large volumes of data (Big Data) in a wide range of applications (Cui, 2016). The Internet of Things (IoT) promises to provide the advantages of the Internet—data exchange, remote control capability, constant connectivity, and so forth—to physical items and services (Almugari *et al.*, 2020).

Product

What satisfies the needs and desires of consumers is the product. A physical object can be considered palpable, as can a service, a concept, or an experience (Carniel, 2022). Products are defined as tangible items that are intended for sale and offer a range of advantages that can be used to satisfy client wants. Selling the product's essence, such as its advantages, practicality, or essential features that business partners seek, is essential when it comes to marketing products. A company's target market is served by a product, which is a combination of commodities and services (Mashur *et al.*, 2019; Klongthong *et al.*, 2020). Because the company sells other items to the market, products play a crucial part in executing the marketing mix (Ma *et al.*, 2020). The product that is supplied to the market must be compatible with the marketing, production, and financial resources, but demand for the product must also be strong enough. To fulfill the wants and demands of customers, a product is created by a business in the form of goods or services. Examples of policies and procedures for products include the kinds of products to be sold, such as quality, design, packaging, and so on, as well as the services to be provided with the product. Two important choice areas are location or distribution channel, which refers to a location or container used to distribute services to target audiences (Gerber *et al.*, 2016). Product development, design, packaging, and other decision-making sectors are examples. According to Ahmad *et al.* (2020), a product development strategy is a set of actions and procedures used to introduce a new product to the market or modify an existing product to launch a new company. The strategy is crucial because it uses market research to create a plan in the event of a product-selling succession. According to Sattyaraksa and Boon-itt (2016), the stages of product development are idea generation, evaluation, editing, prototyping, analysis, product development, market testing, and finally, commercialization. It is also quite common to develop innovations for already-existing products, in which case the stages that are appropriate are a modification of the existing product, value addition of the product, offering a trial, customization and specialization, developing package deals, developing the new product, and finally locating a new market for the product.

Product and Internet of Things (IoT)

The advent of digital technology has facilitated the emergence of a novel array of products within the business sector. Various corporations engage in the process of developing and promoting a diverse range of digital products. The aforementioned goods are specifically tailored to cater to the needs of both commercial and consumer markets. Digital products can be broadly classified into two categories: content and technology. Digital content encompasses various forms of information that are stored and transmitted in a digital format, such as video, audio, text, and images. According to Pogorelova *et al.* (2016), the material is transformed into various business and consumer goods, including newspapers, periodicals, online games, photographs, graphics, and videos. The term "product" pertains to the tangible or intangible offering that is being promoted to consumers by the Internet of Things (IoT) applications, investments, and challenges for enterprises. This offering is intended to be consumed by the target audience of IoT applications for enterprises (Groucutt & Hopkins, 2015). The primary objective of IoT applications for enterprises is to address market needs and demands while also generating demand through the provision of a distinctive and satisfactory customer experience (Stead & Hastings, 2018; Sahaf, 2019). The IoT has an additional potential for the marketing field, as the networked nature of products can generate valuable information that can be utilized to facilitate real-time innovation driven by user preferences. The concept of engaging clients in the development process is referred to by different terms, including user-centric innovation, outside innovation, mass collaboration, wikinomics, or crowdsourcing (Technology Pioneers, 2008). The significance of users as a crucial driver of innovation has been widely acknowledged (Lim, 2017). Furthermore, customers are recognized as a valuable resource for ideas, labor, expertise, and innovation (IBM, 2015). One of the most renowned instances of a user-generated product is Wikipedia, an internet-based encyclopedia. The facilitation of co-creation has mostly been enabled by the Internet, which serves as a medium for connecting individuals. However, the emergence of the Internet of Things has the potential to elevate this phenomenon to an unprecedented extent. In contrast to conventional product development practices, which rely solely on sales data and customer complaints for product design feedback, the utilization of real-time analysis facilitated by machine-to-machine, machine-to-infrastructure, and user-t--machine communication in IoT technology-based products enables a continuous adaptation to evolving circumstances (IBM, 2015).

The deployment of IoT technology presents organizations with opportunities for investment but also poses some problems. These applications provide functional advantages to consumers who utilize the product. The aforementioned functional benefits are both promised and subsequently fulfilled. Nevertheless, it is worth noting that these benefits are also provided by comparable products (Henry, 2018). The primary characteristic that sets apart the IoT technology is the provision of emotional advantages to the consumer, especially such customers who are technology savvy. The products produced and marketed by the IoT technology present organizations with opportunities and obstacles in terms of investments. These products hold the potential to provide consumers with enhanced self-esteem, increased assurance, and heightened security. IoT technology in organizations also holds the potential to satisfy psychological demands related to product consumption. Psychological needs encompass various aspects, such as the requirement for empathy, the necessity for a sense of belonging, and the desire to experience love (Henry, 2018).

Components

The objective of this endeavor is to acquire and construct the most basic arrangement of the IoT technology-based product in order to facilitate prototype examination with minimal expenditure and exertion. This process may entail the design and fabrication of a Printed Circuit Board (PCB), followed by the subsequent integration of the hardware components into the overall system. The components encompassed in this system consist of sensors designed to collect data from the surrounding physical world, a wireless connectivity feature, and LED indications. The data gathered and analyzed by the IoT technology is ultimately utilized by the user *via* devices such as smartphones. At the prototyping stage, the primary objective of the user interface (UI) is to demonstrate the product's worth to the end-user. The accomplishment of this task entails the development of a front-end system that effectively presents the current information provided by the IoT technology.

Social Media

The task at hand involves the conceptualization and development of a design. The concept of the "Internet of Things" (IoT) is pervasive in our surroundings since it involves the integration of intelligent objects equipped with sensors, actuators, and software, together with network connectivity and cloud infrastructure, to facilitate the collection, monitoring, and exchange of data (Fatahi, 2022). There are multiple factors to take into account while creating intelligent and intricate Internet of Things (IoT)-enabled products. In order to meet the requirements of IoT systems, it is imperative that IoT devices include reliable and efficient connectivity, along with advanced data management capabilities and resilient device management features. Connected devices within the realm of the Internet of Things (IoT) are facilitating the acquisition of information at an unprecedented scale. Consequently, this phenomenon is altering the mindset of firms in terms of understanding customer preferences and devising appropriate product designs. IoT gadgets, such as environmental sensors for climate monitoring, wearables for enhancing exercise form, and voice-enabled kitchen appliances, play a significant role in enhancing various aspects of entertainment, health, and society, among other domains (Welch, 2019). The initial iteration of Internet of Things (IoT) devices primarily emphasized the acquisition of external data and its presentation on mobile devices. A limited number of Internet of Things (IoT) products exhibit genuine interaction with their surrounding physical world. Typically, these additions are supplementary features incorporated into pre-existing goods, such as a web-based remote control for television or a web-based interface for managing home climate control systems. The book titled "IoT Product Design and Development" provides a comprehensive introduction to the methodologies, approaches, and optimal strategies required for integrating IoT capabilities into an already existing product or creating whole new IoT goods (Fatahi, 2022). In order to achieve this objective, the volume thoroughly investigates the product design prerequisites pertaining to industrial, business, and consumer contexts. Drawing upon concrete illustrations from the actual world, the book presents a comprehensive framework outlining the process of creation, encompassing valuable insights into optimal approaches and prevalent challenges. According to Fatahi (2022), readers will acquire the necessary knowledge and skills to implement the Internet of Things (IoT) in various industries and professional roles. The book titled "IoT Product Design and Development" serves as a valuable resource for those in the field of mechanical, electrical, and industrial engineering, as well as those working as IoT product managers, business leaders, software and hardware professionals, and data specialists.

Warranty

The concept of warranty refers to a legally binding agreement between a seller and a buyer. The warranty offered by investments in IoT applications presents both opportunities and challenges for enterprises. It encompasses the assurance provided by companies to their customers regarding the performance and quality of the food and services they have purchased (Abratt & Bendixen, 2018). Furthermore, investments and problems related to the Internet of Things (IoT) in enterprises encompass the warranty aspect, which pertains to the reimbursement provided by companies to customers in the event that the product or service fails to meet the advertised benefits and capabilities (Grewal & Levy, 2021). The quality of service needs for an application's development vary depending on the field in which it operates. These requirements encompass a spectrum of options, including best effort, differentiated services (a software-based QoS approach), and guaranteed services (a hardware-based quality of service approach).

PLM

The integration of the Internet of Things (IoT) into the entirety of manufacturing processes is best achieved through the use of Product Lifecycle Management (PLM). According to Išoraitė (2016), the development of IoT necessitates the collaboration of electrical, mechanical, and software design teams in order to ensure timely delivery of goods that align with the intended design. Product lifecycle management (PLM) solutions are purposefully developed to facilitate the integration of all teams and designs into a unified system. This integration fosters enhanced collaboration among teams, expedites design approvals, and augments traceability from the conceptualization stage through initial requirements to the ultimate launch of the product.

Product lifecycle management (PLM) solutions, particularly those that are cloud-based, serve as effective tools for teams to mitigate prevalent challenges associated with requirements, namely the omission of requirements and the development of too complex products. For instance, a corporation operating in the clean technology sector utilized Microsoft Word as a tool for creating and overseeing requirements documents. At the outset, this procedure proved satisfactory in addressing a restricted range of products through the collaboration of a New Product Introduction (NPI) team situated in a singular geographic area (Welch, 2019). Internet of Things (IoT) product lifecycle management (PLM) systems offer enhanced traceability of requirements through direct connections to product design. This is achieved by establishing links between design inputs and design outputs or by establishing links to the relevant section of the product record. The implementation of this integrated requirements method guarantees that if there are modifications to the requirements, both local and dispersed teams are promptly informed in order to assess the potential consequences on subsequent design components, including connection, security, and device management.

The establishment of traceability is necessary in order to maintain the progress and success of product launches. It is crucial to verify that all initial specifications are preserved and in accordance with the final deliverable. To do this, it is recommended to employ suitable test cases for each feature, which should undergo a thorough evaluation and receive approval from all primary stakeholders within the product team. It is imperative to meticulously document and record each step involved in this activity, ensuring that it can be easily referenced and placed within its historical context, particularly in the event that any concerns occur at a later time. The efficacy or inefficacy of any interconnected device is intricately linked to the extent to which requirements are clearly delineated and effectively controlled from the initial stages of product conception. In regulated industries, the utilization of Product Lifecycle Management (PLM) becomes particularly crucial in order to facilitate the establishment of requirements that align with regulatory and safety norms. According to Welch (2019), it has been recognized by forward-thinking IoTs enterprises that effective management of requirements plays a pivotal role in ensuring a prosperous product launch.

Packaging

The implementation of integrated intelligent systems, processes, sensors, data, and analytics is facilitating package makers in making informed decisions, automating operations, and achieving efficiency and cost-saving objectives. These advancements fall within the domain of the IoTs. The packaging of Internet of Things (IoT) devices can be categorized as either active or innovative. Smart packaging encompasses the utilization of sensors and indicators to actively monitor the state of a product, hence facilitating the provision of pertinent information regarding its status. These factors encompass tightness, temperature, freshness, storage time, and other relevant variables (Kucuk, 2017). For example, food packaging has the potential to undergo a color shift as a means of indicating the presence of leaks or contamination by salmonella. Intelligent packaging can be employed to monitor product conditions through several alternative methods. Active packaging refers to a type of packaging that incorporates active components or systems to enhance the quality, safety, and shelf life of the packaged product. Manufacturers employ a range of factors contingent upon the specific product being transported. Among the prevailing options are light-filtering materials, ethylene absorbers, oxygen absorbers, moisture-control mechanisms, antimicrobial coatings, and other such alternatives. An illustrative instance involves the incorporation of oxygen absorbers into the cap of a plastic beer bottle, resulting in an extension of the product's shelf life from three to six months. The primary emphasis of enterprise investments and challenges in the realm of the Internet of Things (IoT) applications lies in the comprehensive consideration of packaging. This entails the meticulous undertaking of designing, evaluating, and developing a container for the products and services that are being produced and promoted (Baines, Fill, & Rosengren, 2017). The advancement of Internet of Things (IoT) technology has led to the emergence of intelligent packaging materials that incorporate embedded sensors. The packaging serves as a medium for conveying information, enabling consumers to interact with it and obtain data that facilitates their optimal utilization of the product. The packaging of the goods, as well as the service provided, enables IoT applications for organizations, which are significant topics of discussion. These applications serve multiple purposes, including facilitating transportation, extending the shelf life of products, and enhancing the overall customer experience (Kareh, 2018). In the realm of packaging, there exists the potential for interactive or technology-driven packaging solutions that enable consumers to engage with products, presenting several advantageous prospects. IoT facilitates the empowerment of various industries through the interconnection of individuals, procedures, and devices, ultimately leading to the improvement of operational efficiency in equipment. A linked packaging system thus not only automates the assembly line but also offers valuable insights that can be utilized to enhance the packaging process for improved performance, alongside numerous other diverse benefits. Historically, the integration of IoT with packaging equipment posed significant challenges due to the prevalent utilization of manually controlled gear and outdated automation systems. According to Deepak and Jeyakumar (2019), the existing systems were not originally intended to be compatible with contemporary Internet of Things (IoT) technologies, necessitating expensive updates and customized development efforts. In contemporary times, it is possible to enhance packages by integrating minuscule electronic components that bestow additional functionality. Several examples of technological devices commonly used in various applications include Bluetooth, alarm systems, RFID chips, LED lights, and loudspeakers. These various components engage in communication in order to fulfill their protective role and offer notable conveniences in each context where they are employed. In the present era, the decrease in expenses and increased accessibility of diverse, flexible IoT technologies have significantly transformed the aforementioned scenario. Numerous enterprises possess expertise in the domain of IoTs, hence rendering the integration of IoT into existing equipment more economically viable. According to Kucuk (2017), contemporary IoT sensors offer cost-effective, high-performance, and resilient capabilities, hence presenting the packaging industry with a diverse range of innovative solutions. The incorporation of IoT sensors within the manufacturing facility's packaging operations and inventory management system enables users to obtain immediate and practical insights through the utilization of data analytics. The data that is gathered assists individuals in promptly addressing any unforeseen issues that may arise in real time within the operational environment, hence ensuring smooth and uninterrupted production processes. The user possesses the ability to examine the acquired insights and afterward make crucial decisions pertaining to the improvement of corporate operations, optimization of employee productivity, and effective administration of the workplace. The key to addressing these challenges lies in the implementation of a comprehensive IoT asset management platform that is capable of seamlessly supporting a diverse range of devices, networks, protocols, and cloud environments. There are several advantages associated with the implementation of the IoT technology in packaging systems.

Customer Engagement

The concept of customer engagement refers to the active involvement and interaction between a customer and a company. It encompasses various strategies and techniques employed by the firm. Smart packaging facilitates communication between the consumer and the product. The utilization of new content, entertainment, and the elicitation of emotional engagement are potential benefits that can be derived from it. Enhancing the level of interaction and connection between brands and customers has been found to have a positive impact on both sales performance and the development of brand loyalty.

Innovation

The concept of innovation is a critical aspect of various academic disciplines and industries. Organizations have the potential to enhance their capacity for innovation and introduce more influential products and services to the market. The enhancement of profitability presents novel prospects for innovation and the enhancement of valuation. This innovation enables organizations to identify and leverage competitive advantages, explore new revenue prospects, enhance customer connections, and achieve greater operational efficiency.

Customer Empowerment

The concept of customer empowerment refers to the process of granting customers the ability to exert influence and control over their interactions with businesses or service.

Intelligent packaging provides a notable user interface that may be utilized to acquire additional information regarding the purchased goods. By scanning a QR code on a food package, customers can get information pertaining to dietary considerations, ingredient analysis, and nutritional content.

Exposing the Utilization of the Product

By establishing a connection between the package and the cloud, brands are able to access a substantial amount of data. This includes the initial opening of the package, future openings and closings, the location and frequency of usage, and additional relevant details.

Quality Control

The concept of quality control refers to the systematic processes and procedures implemented within an organization to ensure that products or services meet or exceed established. The design of packaging can be utilized to facilitate the monitoring of a product's condition. It has the potential to tell whether a situation is favorable or compromised. The outcome entails enhanced accessibility to authentic, high-quality products directly from the producer. The implementation of thermal and video sensors within the manufacturing line facilitates the assurance of precise adherence to standards for each unit produced. The technology possesses the capability to rapidly detect instances of product misalignment, flaws, and other forms of errors. Manufacturers employing this technology are relieved from concerns regarding quality issues, and notably, they possess the capability to modify data settings, hence enabling the system to conduct quality checks on novel product lines.

Experience

The term "experience" refers to the knowledge, skills, and understanding of an individual. IoT leads to the optimization of user experience to provide seamless interaction. The implementation of intelligent packaging enhances the user-friendliness of the product. Enhancements in instructional clarity can be achieved through the inclusion of video links or the provision of online chat functionality, enabling users to seek individualized assistance and address any inquiries they may have. The investments and challenges associated with IoT applications in organizations' products aim to enhance the customers' consumption experience, offering them a distinct and outstanding encounter (Kotler & Keller, 2021). This particular experience encompasses client engagement with products, resulting in diverse and favorable emotional responses. Furthermore, it aids organizations in upholding their distinctiveness in the face of competition, contributing to the preservation of investments and addressing issues associated with Internet of Things (IoT) applications (Varadarajan, 2015; Kotabe & Helsen, 2020).

Demand

The proliferation of Internet of Things (IoT) technology has necessitated that company operations adapt and align with market demand. The impact of the global market compels numerous industries to reassess their strategies, processes, and general approaches to operations management, with a particular focus on productivity and quality (Park, 2020). The concept of Industry 4.0, which represents the future of manufacturing, aims to incorporate various principles and strategies such as just-in-time (JIT), total quality management (TQM), computer-integrated manufacturing (CIM), agile manufacturing, lean production, quick respond manufacturing (QRM), and supply chain management (SCM) (Gunasekaran *et al.*, 2012).

Brand

The concept of a brand refers to a unique and identifiable symbol, name, and design. Enterprises invest in generating brands out of their products and service offerings within the realm of Internet of Things (IoT) applications. This entails allocating resources towards establishing and enhancing their brand identity in relation to IoT-based products and services. Brands are also actively participating in this phenomenon. Due to its potential to enhance the user-friendliness of products, gather customer data, and maintain competitiveness in a dynamic market, this phenomenon offers significant opportunities for companies. The concept of connectedness and smart applications is frequently examined within the framework of enhancing consumer satisfaction, including various aspects such as gadgets, smart homes, and intelligent appliances (Kucuk, 2017). The advantages of interconnected systems in relation to business outcomes encompass cost reduction, operational streamlining, and generation of additional revenue. There is substantial evidence to support the transformation of consumer spaces and the influence on financial performance as a result of the Internet of Things (IoT). This evidence has garnered attention from several industries. Therefore, it is not unexpected to observe numerous brands embracing the Internet of Things (IoT) trend. Consumer impression is positively influenced, brand efficiency is enhanced, creativity and experimentation among customers are promoted, and preferences are established. This implies that enterprises investing in IoT applications face the task of engaging in brand-building endeavors for their offerings. These endeavors involve associating distinct designs and communications with their products to achieve differentiation and facilitate effective communication with the intended audience (Gillespie & Swan, 2021). The branding-building operations carried out by firms investing in Internet of Things (IoT) applications aim to enhance the target audience's connection with the services (Abratt & Bendixen, 2018). According to Kareh (2018), investments and problems related to Internet of Things (IoT) applications in organizations can lead to increased customer loyalty, repeat purchases, and a positive view of the company's offers. In order to achieve exceptional performance, a brand must possess the necessary proficiency in the field of the Internet of Things (IoT) and be capable of effectively acquiring, categorizing, retaining, and analyzing substantial volumes of data. Currently, companies are allocating significant percentages of their financial resources towards the incorporation of Internet of Things (IoT) technology into their operations. Consequently, there is a growing demand for professionals with specialized knowledge and skills in this domain (Khan, 2014).

Quality of Products and Services

Indeed, the efficient application of manufacturing automation necessitates adherence to high-quality requirements pertaining to robustness, dependability, and latency. The IoT architecture can be conceptualized as consisting of various layers that facilitate support, maintenance, and deployment at a higher level. However, it is important for IoT systems to maintain consistent basic operations, which are contingent upon the application domain and necessitate multiple quality factors. Various implementation ideas and concepts are employed to define the architectures of the IoTs in terms of service quality. These include the utilization of appropriate protocols and access networks to implement IoT systems based on service-oriented architectures. The quality of a product in terms of its performance, durability, and overall satisfaction for the consumer. The investments and problems associated with Internet of Things (IoT) applications in organizations mostly pertain to the company's ability to effectively meet the requirements and desires of customers through its range of products and services (Baines, Fill, & Rosengren, 2017; Deepak & Jeyakumar, 2019). Furthermore, the quality of the product for The investments and challenges related to the applications of the Internet of Things (IoT) for enterprises encompass various aspects, such as the company's commitment to industry standards and benchmarks, as well as the comprehensive fulfillment of its intended meaning and purpose (Iacobucci, 2021; Groucutt & Hopkins, 2015; Chernev, 2018). According to Henry (2018), organizations face both investments and obstacles in relation to the applications of the Internet of Things (IoT), which ultimately contribute to the maintenance of excellent product quality. The maintenance of high product quality is achieved by the strategic addition of value at various levels within the value chain. According to Henry (2018), organizations engaged in the procurement of raw materials for Internet of Things (IoT) applications prioritize sourcing from suppliers that are both reputable and trusted. The raw materials undergo processing within meticulously controlled settings to ensure the products keep a consistently high level of quality. The provision of high-quality promise and delivery offers organizations a unique competitive edge in terms of investments and problems related to the Internet of Things (IoT) applications. Ravi and colleagues (2018) have provided an explanation of the significance of Quality of Service (QoS) in the context of the Internet of Things (IoT). The authors have provided a concise overview of the service quality parameters and metrics that should be taken into account at each layer. The authors have categorized the extant literature on the Internet of Things (IoT) based on many study themes, including standardization, system architecture and performance, and service quality, among others.

The Characteristics/Features and Capabilities

Product features or characteristics encompass the distinct traits and attributes exhibited in the offerings of the Internet of Things (IoT) Applications investments and challenges for enterprises, enabling the organization to effectively provide unparalleled value to customers through the production and provision of products and services (Varadarajan, 2015; Kotler & Keller, 2021). The inclusion of product qualities and features enables organizations to establish points of difference for their offerings within the context of Internet of Things (IoT) applications. This strategic approach is crucial for enterprises to effectively address the investments and issues associated with IoT implementation (Kotler & Keller, 2021; Park, 2020). According to Abratt and Bendixen (2018), organizations face investments and issues in the realm of Internet of Things (IoT) applications. These investments and challenges are aimed at ensuring that the manufactured product effectively serves its intended purpose and aligns with customer expectations. The investments and problems associated with Internet of Things (IoT) applications for organizations mostly revolve around product design and its ability to effectively meet consumer expectations and address market gaps (Baines, Fill, & Rosengren, 2017).

Product Style

The investments and problems associated with Internet of Things (IoT) applications in companies necessitate a deliberate emphasis on product design and aesthetics, as well as the product's capacity to align with the expectations and lifestyle of the intended target audience (Groucutt & Hopkins, 2015). The investments and problems associated with the applications of the Internet of Things (IoT) in companies necessitate the alignment of product style and design with its intended features and purpose.

The Factors of Efficiency and Accessibility

Convenience is a key aspect of consideration for organizations when investing in and addressing the issues of The Internet of Things (IoT) applications in their product offerings. The investments and challenges associated with the applications of the Internet of Things (IoT) in organizations are focused on ensuring that the products and services provided are user-friendly and convenient. The factor of convenience enables organizations to experience a higher rate of consumption, improved sales, and trials in their investments and issues related to the Internet of Things (IoT) applications (Kotabe & Helsen, 2020; Kucuk, 2017). The investments and challenges associated with Internet of Things (IoT) applications in organizations are aimed at ensuring the availability of their product and service offerings to target consumers through diverse retail setups. The widespread accessibility of the Internet of Things (IoT) applications, investments, and challenges for enterprises enables consumers to conveniently acquire their offerings from diverse locations, thereby granting the Internet of Things (IoT) applications, investments, and challenges for enterprises a competitive edge over rival entities (Chernev, 2018).

The Provision of After-sales Service

The investments and challenges associated with Internet of Things (IoT) applications in organizations pertain to addressing post-sales inquiries and consumer expectations, encompassing procedures for returns and exchanges, and the post-purchase support provided by the company. The investments and problems associated with Internet of Things (IoT) applications are of significant importance for organizations, as they play a crucial role in determining consumer satisfaction with the offerings provided (Iacobucci, 2021; Chernev, 2018).

The Level of User-friendliness

The goods produced and marketed by the Internet of Things (IoT) applications entail a user-friendly interface, hence facilitating ease of use for organizations. According to Henry (2018), every product is accompanied by a user manual that is designed to be easily comprehensible and offers straightforward guidance on product utilization. Consumers have the option to contact the 24/7 hotline in order to obtain comprehensive information regarding the utilization of the product.

Additionally, shop staff offer comprehensive instructions and explanations pertaining to the utilization of the product during the point of purchase.

The Product Line Length within the Realm of IoT Commerce

The determination pertaining to the product line necessitates careful consideration of the interplay between the intricacy of existing items and the corresponding service demands, as well as the extent of untapped market opportunities (Yen & Yao, 2018). In the current analysis, it is recommended that IoT commerce maintains its existing item mix instead of embarking on the introduction of new products to broaden its product line.

The topic of discussion pertains to the product line depth within the realm of IoT commerce.

The authors, Yen and Yao (2018), discuss the determinations pertaining to the quantity of distinct Stock Keeping Units (SKU) for a specific product. As an illustration, Apple offers its iPhone in a range of colors despite the hardware and software components remaining consistent.

Various Stock-keeping Units (SKUs)

IoT presents a range of solutions that cater to corporations of all sizes. Enterprises have utilized various stock-keeping units (SKUs) to enhance market penetration in the realm of Internet of Things (IoT) applications. This has resulted in expenditures and obstacles, as discussed by Henry (2018). Various SKUs can be acquired and utilized according to the consumption requirements of customers and the specific target markets. The trial rate for organizations has increased due to the manufacture of many SKUs and the investments and problems associated with Internet of Things (IoT) applications. The utilization of various stock-keeping units (SKUs) has been significant in enhancing the accessibility of products for firms investing in Internet of Things (IoT) applications (Henry, 2018). IoT applications are characterized by diverse stock-keeping units (SKUs) in the available product range. The availability of various SKU sizes for products offered by enterprises in the IoT applications industry serves as a means to enhance sales. This is due to the fact that different customer segments exhibit varying demands for product quantity, influenced by factors such as usage patterns, income levels, and lifestyle preferences (Grewal & Levy, 2021; Deepak & Jeyakumar, 2019).

The Fulfillment of Customer Demand

The fulfillment of customer demands, the achievement of its intended purpose, and the efficient and effective functioning of a product and service are crucial aspects of product quality in the context of investments and challenges related to the Internet of Things (IoT) applications for enterprises (Iacobucci, 2021; Deepak & Jeyakumar, 2019). According to Wu and Li (2018), organizations strategically invest in Internet of Things (IoT) applications to address the difficulties and opportunities associated with the IoT. By effectively managing internal expenses, enterprises may ensure the availability of their products to customers at competitive pricing.

The Breadth of Firms' Portfolio

According to Henry (2018), organizations face a wide range of investments and challenges in relation to the applications of the Internet of Things (IoT). This field encompasses a diverse portfolio of products. The diverse range of applications inside the Internet of Things (IoT) presents both opportunities and obstacles for organizations seeking to engage in various market segments. Moreover, the diverse range of investments in the Internet of Things (IoT) applications contributes to the financial stability of organizations while also presenting various obstacles. The inclusion of a wider range of products in the portfolio enhances the value of investments and presents additional hurdles for organizations involved in the Internet of Things (IoT) applications.

Implications

The practical application of the marketing mix is a strategic approach involving personalized product recommendations that directly contribute to enhancing the operational efficiency of a commercial organization. This is achieved through increased sales and profits, as well as fostering consumer loyalty towards the company. The reason for this phenomenon is that when implementing the trade service advice, the buyer becomes aware of the company's responsiveness to such requests, which is characterized by individualized and high-quality service. It is imperative for product directors to engage in working together with different divisions in order to effectively utilize the Framework. Furthermore, they should engage in multiple iterations throughout all levels of the system until a cohesive and unified solution is achieved. Comprehending data generated by the Internet of Things (IoT) necessitates more than the mere development of extensive data and applications on a large scale. In order to fully leverage the potential of the Internet of Things (IoT), companies must possess a comprehensive understanding of the storage location for the vast amount of data generated by IoT machines, as well as the associated challenges and issues. In addition, firms require more comprehensive and sophisticated data analytics solutions in order to enhance their operational efficiency and overall effectiveness. In order to harness the potential benefits of the Internet of Things (IoT), organizations must not only seek to gain valuable insights regarding customers, employees, and manufacturing facilities but also address the crucial tasks of data storage, analytics, and conversion. This process is essential for transforming raw data into meaningful information and knowledge, enabling organizations to make efficient and effective decisions. The share of workloads in data centers dedicated to processing massive quantities of IoT data in real time is expected to grow, posing new problems in terms of security, scalability, and analytics for providers. In order to effectively manage the intricacies of a manufacturing network, it is imperative to possess a future-oriented leadership style and mindset. The implementation of IoT technology has proven to be advantageous for brands, as it facilitates improvements in productivity, efficiency, and security. Consequently, it is anticipated that this technological advancement will contribute to a prosperous period for brands.

CONCLUSION

The product includes both production and end-use items, which are distributed through conventional logistical routes. Additionally, it comprises information products and services that are given through Internet channels. Furthermore, online stores offer trade and information services. Active involvement in the process of developing new products, along with the pursuit of innovation, can contribute to the success and performance of an organization within the market. The development, invention, and attainment of high performance in products require significant effort and are not readily achieved. Connectivity facilitates the integration of smart items into a broader ecosystem of products, processes, and individuals, which undergo organic transformations as users provide data. With the continuous evolution of IoT product design and its associated technologies, the future development of IoT products will capitalize on the substantial quantities of actionable data generated by these devices. This will enable increased digital connectivity in our world.

REFERENCES

Abratt, R., Bendixen, M. (2018). *Strategic marketing: Concepts and cases.* New York, United States: Routledge.
[http://dx.doi.org/10.4324/9780429489327]

Ahmad, F., Mustapa, Z., Ilyas, B., & Halim Perdana Kusuma, A. (2020). Relationship of TQM on Managerial Performance: Evidence from Property Sector in Indonesia. 47–57.

Almugari, F., Bajaj, P., Tabash, M. I., Khan, A., & Ali M. A. (2020). An examination of consumers' adoption of internet of things (IoT) in Indian banks. *Cogent Business & Management*, 7:1, 1809071.
[http://dx.doi.org/10.1080/23311975.2020.1809071]

Baines, P., Fill, C., Rosengren, S. (2017). *Marketing.*. New York, United States: Oxford University Press.

Chernev, A. (2018). *Strategic marketing management.* Berlin/Heidelberg, Germany: Cerebellum Press.

Cui, X. (2016). *The internet of things. In Ethical Ripples of Creativity and Innovation.* (pp. 61-68). London: Palgrave Macmillan.

Carniel, A. (2022). The ultimate guide to marketing mix: 4Ps, 7Ps, 8Ps, 4Cs, 7Cs. Available from: https://www.albertocarniel.com/post/marketing-mix.

Chen, B.W., Ji, W. (2016). Intelligent Marketing in Smart Cities: Crowdsourced Data for Geo-Conquesting. *IT Prof., 18*(4), 18-24.
[http://dx.doi.org/10.1109/MITP.2016.64]

Deepak, R., Jeyakumar, S. (2019). *Marketing management.* New Delhi, India: Educreation Publishing.

Firman, A., Putra, A.H.P.K., Mustapa, Z., Ilyas, G.B., Karim, K. (2020). Re-conceptualization of Business Model for Marketing Nowadays: Theory and Implications. The Journal of Asian Finance. *Economics and Business, 7*(7), 279-291. [JAFEB].

Gerber, C., Ward, S., Goedhals-Gerber, L. (2014). The impact of perceived risk on on-line purchase behaviour. *Risk Governance and Control: Financial Markets and Institutions, 4*(4), 99-106.
[http://dx.doi.org/10.22495/rgcv4i4c1art4]

Gunasekaran, A., Eric, W.T. (2012). Ngai. The future of operations management: an outlook and analysis *Int. J. Prod. Econ., 135*(2), 687-701.

Gillespie, K., Swan, K. (2021). *Global marketing.* New York, United States: Routledge.
[http://dx.doi.org/10.4324/9781003141709]

Grewal, D., Levy, M. (2021). *M: marketing.* New York, United States: McGraw-Hill Education.

Guo, B., Zhang, D., Wang, Z., Yu, Z., Zhou, X. (2013). Opportunistic IoT: Exploring the harmonious interaction between human and the internet of things. *J. Netw. Comput. Appl., 36*(6), 1531-1539.
[http://dx.doi.org/10.1016/j.jnca.2012.12.028]

Gupta, A., Tsai, T., Rueb, D., Yamaji, M., Middleton, P., (2017). Forecast: Internet of Things — Endpoints and Associated Services, Worldwide, 2017. Gartner. Retrieved at: https://www.gartner.com/en/documents/3840665/forecast-internet-of-things (Accessed 16 May 2020).

Marjani, M., Nasaruddin, F., Gani, A., Karim, A., Hashem, I.A.T., Siddiqa, A., Yaqoob, I. (2017). Big IoT data analytics: architecture, opportunities, and open research challenges. *IEEE Access, 5*, 5247-5261.
[http://dx.doi.org/10.1109/ACCESS.2017.2689040]

Henry, Z. (2018). Marketing Mix Of The Internet of Things IoT Applications investments and challenges for enterprises. Available from: https://www.case48.com/case/The-Internet-of-Things-IoT-Applications-investments-and-challenges-for-enterprises-Marketing-Mix-19646.

IBM (2015). The impact of the Internet of Things on product development. IBM Corp.

Kareh, A. (2018). Evolution of the four Ps: Revisiting the marketing mix. Retrieved June 2022, Available from: https://www.forbes.com/sites/forbesagencycouncil/2018/01/03/evolution-of-the-four-ps-revisiti-g-the-marketing-mix/.

Khan, M. (2014). The concept of 'marketing mix'and its elements. *Int. J. Inf. Bus. Manag., 6*(2), 95-107.

Kotabe, M., Helsen, K. (2020). *Global marketing management.* Hoboken, New Jersey, United States: John Wiley & Sons.

Kotler, P., Keller, K. (2021). *Marketing Management (15th global edition).* London, United Kingdom: Pearson Education Limited.

Klongthong, W., Thavorn, J., Watcharadamrongkun, S., Ngamkroeckjoti, C. (2020). Determination of Factors in Cultural Dimensions and SERVQUAL Model Affecting the Corporate Image of Pharmacy Retail Stores. The Journal of Asian Finance. *Economics and Business, 7*(10), 875-884.

Kumar, J., Nayak, J.K. (2018). Brand community relationships transitioning into brand relationships:

Mediating and moderating mechanisms. *J. Retailing Consum. Serv.,* *45*(January), 64-73. [http://dx.doi.org/10.1016/j.jretconser.2018.08.007]

Kusuma, A.H.P., Sudirman, A., Purnomo, A., Aisyah, S., Sahir, S.H., Rumondang, A., Salmiah, S., Halim, F., Wirapraja, A., Napitupulu, D. (2020). *Brand Management: Esensi, Posisi dan Strategi..* Yayasan Kita Menulis.

Kucuk, S. (2017). Marketing and Marketing Mix.*Visualizing Marketing..* London, United Kingdom: Palgrave Macmillan.
[http://dx.doi.org/10.1007/978-3-319-48027-5_2]

Lim, W.M. (2017). Online group buying: Some insights from the business-to-business perspective. *Ind. Mark. Manage.,* *65*(March), 182-193.
[http://dx.doi.org/10.1016/j.indmarman.2017.03.011]

Liu, Y., Jiang, C., Zhao, H. (2019). Assessing product competitive advantages from the perspective of customers by mining user-generated content on social media. *Decis. Support Syst.,* *123*, 113079.
[http://dx.doi.org/10.1016/j.dss.2019.113079]

Fitriany, Gunawan, B.I., Ashoer, M., Hidayat, M., Perdana, H., Putra, K. (2019). Moving From Traditional to Society 5.0: Case study by Online Transportation Business. *Journal of Distribution Science,* *17*(9), 93-102.
[http://dx.doi.org/10.15722/jds.17.9.201909.93]

Pogorelova, E.V., Yakhneeva, I.V., Agafonovaa, A.N., Prokubovskaya, A.O. (2016). Marketing Mix for E-commerce. *Int. J. Environ. Sci. Educ.,* *11*(14), 6744-6759.

Park, S. (2020). *Marketing management (Vol. 3). Retrieved June 2022,* Available from: https://books.google.com.pk/books/about/Marketing_Management.html?id=p6v7DwAAQBAJ&redir_esc=y.

Stead, M., Hastings, G. (2018). Advertising in the social marketing mix: getting the balance right.*Social Marketing.* (pp. 29-43). London, England: Psychology Press.
[http://dx.doi.org/10.4324/9781315805795-3]

Varadarajan, R. (2015). Strategic marketing, marketing strategy and market strategy. *AMS Rev.,* *5*(3-4), 78-90.
[http://dx.doi.org/10.1007/s13162-015-0073-9]

Welch, P. (July 31, 2019). *IoT & the Product Development Process.* Available from: https://www.automation.com/en-us/articles/2019/iot-the-product-development-process.

Wu, Y.L., Li, E.Y. (2018). Marketing mix, customer value, and customer loyalty in social commerce. *Internet Res.,* *28*(1), 74-104.
[http://dx.doi.org/10.1108/IntR-08-2016-0250]

Yen, B., Yao, Y. (2018). *The Internet of Things (IoT)..* Shaping the Future of e-Commerce Harvard Business Review Case Study. Published by HBR Publications.

CHAPTER 3

Internet of Things (IoT) and Pricing

S. Jayadatta[1,*], **Mohammed Majeed**[2], **Seidu Alhassan**[3] and **Sulemana Anas**[2]

[1] *KLE's Institute of Management Studies and Research (IMSR), Karnataka, India*

[2] *Department of Marketing, Tamale Technical University, Tamale, Ghana*

[3] *Secretaryship and Management Department, Tamale Technical University, Tamale, Ghana*

Abstract: The Internet of Things (IoT) is a rapidly expanding network of interconnected computing devices that have recently attracted the attention of governments and businesses. There is no need for human interaction when using the IoT. The medical, transportation, and automotive industries have been among the first to take advantage of some of the most innovative uses of the Internet of Things. Although it is the only part of the marketing mix that actually generates revenue, price is also crucial. Therefore, this chapter explores how IoT can be used to determine the best pricing strategy for a company's goods and services.

Keywords: Internet of Things, IoT, Internet, Price, Pricing, Technology.

INTRODUCTION

Intelligent sensors, often known as Internet of Things devices, are essentially handheld computers. The term "Internet of Things" refers to the network of physical computers, mechanical or digital devices equipped with software, sensors, and processing ability that are connected to one another and the internet in order to share and receive data and information. Any living creature, human or otherwise, with an implanted technology that can be read by another person or that can communicate with another IoT device can be considered a thing in the Internet of Things (Williams, 2022). This information is then sent from the device *via* an IP network, such as the Internet. This is after it has been compiled from a wide variety of hard data sources. Depending on the task at hand, the sensor may also include amplifiers, filters, and converters. Battery-operated gadgets with unique Internet Protocol (IP) addresses power the Internet of Things. Most sensor readings are sent to a central hub or gateway in the Internet of Things. Data is rou-

---

* **Corresponding author S. Jayadatta:** KLE's Institute of Management Studies and Research (IMSR), Karnataka, India; E-mail: jayadattaster@gmail.com

tinely filtered and normalized by IoT gateways. Raw sensor data is typically collected and organized by the IoT gateway.

Traditional methods of advertising are also being disrupted by the Internet of Things. Personalized information, tailored advertising messages, and sales promotion offers are only some of the ways that retail establishments, sales networks, public utilities, and outdoor advertising suppliers have utilized IoT technology, as noted by Mittal (2012). In the near future, consumers will only receive filtered message content tailored to their specific requirements and interests, whether they access the information through conventional means of communication or *via* smart devices such as smart refrigerators. Customers will no longer be subjected to intrusive advertising that could detract from their overall experience. Therefore, businesses can mitigate customer complaints about generic advertising through the IoT. With the ability to communicate with users of a wide variety of smart devices, there is a chance to track and analyze their actions and to keep businesses proactively oriented toward providing satisfying customer service. It provides companies with an almost boundless window of opportunity to learn about their consumers' wants and requirements and respond appropriately and promptly. In addition, it is said that IoT can completely change how businesses interact with their customers. The breadth of reciprocal connections will expand beyond the human-centric paradigm as customers can interact with smart items, and objects can operate together as assemblages through a process of ongoing interaction (Hoffman & Novak, 2018).

The Internet of Things is used to process and store this massive amount of data and information on the cloud. Insights gained from this are used to further tailor advertising campaigns to individual consumers. Internet of Things (IoT) solutions are being used in today's businesses for a wide variety of purposes, including customer support, sales, and market research (Williams, 2022). All of this information is put to good use by analyzing user patterns and serving up more relevant ads and content. Data and network traffic are both impacted by the Internet of Things; therefore, it takes specialized knowledge to manage both effectively and derive value from them. Thanks to the Internet of Things, businesses can better understand their customers' regular purchase processes. This allows for more effective transmission of marketing messages at the appropriate stage of the buyer's journey (Williams, 2022). The Internet of Things is assisting businesses in growing and improving their offerings to customers. The Internet of Things is helping companies connect globally and share marketing data (including pricing, product, promotion, and location). This chapter looks at the application of IoT in the price and pricing of company products.

LITERATURE

IoT in Marketing

In 1985, at a Congressional Black Caucus Foundation wireless session supported by the FCC, Peter Lewis first used the word. At the time, he defined IoT as "the integration of people, processes, and technology with connectable devices and sensors." While Lewis's words did not catch on right away, by the late '90s and early 2000s, the concept of an interconnected network of everyday objects became increasingly mainstream. The Internet of Things (IoT) was conceived as a way to improve people's daily lives by allowing objects to quickly and remotely respond to their needs and requests. In recent years, the technology has gained momentum thanks to the proliferation of wearable and smart gadgets like the light and door home sensors we are all getting used to.

Marketers who can extract actionable insights from this wealth of data and insights into customer behavior will always be ahead of the competition (Williams, 2022). Because of the wealth of information made available by the Internet of Things (IoT), modern marketing is more data-driven. They make use of previously unavailable data and information about customers' device interactions and use it to make personalized outreach. They take in essential information, learn about the customer's purchasing process, and tailor the experience to the individual. By integrating their products in a smart way, they are able to meet their consumers' demands at the moment with relevant material and messages (Williams, 2022). With the use of IoT, marketers will be sure to deliver individualized communications regarding remedies to our respective problems, whether it be dandruff or hair loss. The Internet of Things has made it easier for salespeople to close deals and for customers to have their problems resolved in record time. Smart CRM (Customer Relationship Management) systems are used by marketers to sort through the deluge of data they get and organize it in real-time. Faster sales closure and greater levels of customer satisfaction are the result (Porter & Heppelmann, 2014). Nowadays, communication between organizations and departments is usually swift and painless. As an added bonus, this enables marketers to instantly adapt their messaging in response to customer purchases from other businesses.

Price/Pricing

A good or service's price is the amount that customers must pay to acquire it. It is the cost to the buyer in exchange for the benefits promised by the seller and the cost to the seller in exchange for the offering. What buyers are ready to give up in terms of time or effort is considered part of the price (Carniel, 2022). Since price is the only variable that can actually turn a profit, it plays a pivotal role in any marketing strategy. Expenses arise from the remaining elements of the marketing mix. Sales volume and, by extension, a company's bottom line are closely related to a product's price. Important elements that influence pricing include supply and demand, costs, competitive pricing, and government regulations. In most cases, a product's price does not correspond with its actual value. To encourage exclusivity or broaden availability, prices might be set higher or lower, respectively.

Price Internet of Things

Although IoT shifts competition away from price alone, it nevertheless presents opportunities and difficulties to marketers when setting prices for their products. Companies can more effectively capture value through pricing when they have insight into how customers are using the product (Porter, Heppelmann, 2014). Companies gain valuable insight into the whereabouts of their merchandise when sensors are built inside their goods. Companies can now set rates based on customers' actual usage patterns thanks to the information provided by these behavioral analytics (Chui, Löffler, Roberts, 2010). Cost, customer value, and competitive analysis form the basis of the pricing strategy. However, data from the most successful online retailers suggests new, innovative approaches to dynamic pricing and customization are emerging (Pogorelova *et al.*, 2016). Because of the Internet of Things, prices in online commerce can be very variable and responsive to market conditions, and pricing tactics might take on a unique flavor for each user. Gaining market share through competitive pricing or price changes in response to demand is one pricing strategy. Some companies might drop their prices thanks to increased efficiency and the resulting decrease in operating expenses. When a company can reach and serve its clients with fewer staff, fewer physical locations, and more technological means, it can save money. When consumers can use the internet to facilitate their search and purchase, they save time, effort, and money. Customer expectations that costs should be cheaper online than in-store make pricing considerations more important for an online business (Harris & Dennis,2002). The internet empowers consumers to bargain harder. Price information from several vendors is readily available to consumers. Intelligent shopping agents are software-based search tools that provide product and pricing information to customers. With IoT, pricing methods are about to reach new heights. Smart, connected devices typically have greater fixed costs due to upfront technological design and more sophisticated product designs, making companies susceptible to pricing pressure (Porter, Heppelmann, 2015). As a result of IoT, not only will there be more customer data available, allowing for more precise dynamic pricing, but new methods of monetization will also appear. This creates the difficulty of ensuring profitability through the sale of anything else than a single, comprehensive offering. The price that customers are willing to pay for the service or product provided by the Internet of Things IoT applications, investments, and difficulties for organizations is an important part of the marketing mix. The pricing strategy and the price of the offerings are crucial because they directly affect the company's profit levels and revenue (Kotabe & Helsen, 2020; Deepak & Jeyakumar, 2019). This is especially true for investments in and challenges posed by IoT applications for enterprises

ROI

By leveraging IoT technology, businesses may reap the benefits of the product-a--a-service revenue model. Businesses can monitor the whereabouts and utilization of rented equipment. With a lease-like approach, businesses may avoid upfront costs while still keeping tabs on relevant information through a centralized dashboard. Customer return on investment (ROI) can be positively affected by such Internet of Things asset tracking and monitoring solutions (Jennifer, 2022).

Discounts

Discounts on products and services are one way that businesses adapt their pricing strategies to account for the investments and problems posed by IoT applications in the business world. To attract customers, attract interest, or even discharge surplus inventory and supply to increase sales (Baines, Fill, & Rosengren, 2017), the price of products and services is often discounted in the Internet of Things IoT applications, investments, and challenges for enterprises.

Subscription

Subscription pricing has been increasingly common in recent years. Subscription plans allow businesses to provide savings for multi-year commitments. The monthly fee is the same for all subscribers regardless of how often they utilize the service. By incorporating pricing models into IoT infrastructure, businesses can charge customers more or less based on their actual consumption. The new pricing model charges clients based on their actual consumption (Jennifer, 2022).

Connivance and Deceit

Providers can either compete with one another or work together to purchase sensing data from sensors and sell services to end customers. Given the strategies of competing providers, a service provider will determine its selling price and subscription fee in order to maximize its own profit (Minerva *et al.*, 2015). As an alternative, the service providers might band together to increase their bottom line. Research into market collusion and its prevention is possible.

Margins

Internet of Things (IoT) applications, investments, and challenges for enterprises allow for margins by charging more than the true cost of producing a good or service, thereby creating a profit for the business (Kucuk, 2017). Internet of Things (IoT) Applications investments and problems for businesses are heavily reliant on the offering's quality and the company's brand equity and brand value.

Goodness of the Data

The suppliers might set a different selling price for each sensor to motivate them to produce accurate readings. For example, sensors can maximize profit by minimizing the cost and effort involved in gathering, processing, and sending data to the service provider, therefore improving the overall data quality. For instance, using a camera as a sensor can result in higher quality video capture, but at the expense of increased power requirements and data transfer rates. Therefore, until the price is really high, the camera will not do it. Models that simultaneously optimize pricing and performance are feasible, as shown by Minerva *et al.* (2015).

Means of Exchange

The payment options provided by a business are a major consideration in the pricing strategy for The Internet of Things IoT Applications investments and problems for organizations (Kotler & Keller, 2021; Abratt & Bendixen, 2018). The Internet of Things (IoT) applications, investments, and challenges for organizations ensure the inclusion of various payment methods as it primarily handles distribution to retail *via* agents and merchants. All forms of payment are included, from digital to cash to credit (Grewal & Levy, 2021; Groucutt & Hopkins, 2015).

Sensors

In response to shifts in the market, both sensors and consumers can modify their reservation wages and reservation prices. To find the optimal reservation salary and reservation price, an auction may be a useful technique. It is possible to create a pricing system that discriminates.

Market-Based Pricing

By calculating its production costs and adding a markup proportionate to the return it seeks, IoT Commerce can use a cost-based pricing strategy. The method may not work in a highly competitive market with variable pricing. Based on its remaining power, resource utilization, and packet-sending prices, the device then calculates the total cost of communicating with its neighbors. The gadget will choose a neighbor with the lowest total cost based on the calculated selling prices and profits (Minerva, Biru, & Rotondi, 2015). When compared to a local taxi service that is not backed by private equity and a long-term strategy, Uber, which is losing billions of dollars every year, can offer lower costs and survive.

Skimming the Market with Prices

IoT commerce may charge more for popular products because consumers are willing to pay more for them.

Competitive Pricing

By providing an affordable balance of product features, quality, and service *via* IoT and a stripped-down version of the product, users can get a feel for the product at a price they can afford.

High-End Costs

Some of the product lines in "The Internet of Things: IoT Applications, Investments and Challenges for Enterprises" are priced higher than their competitors in order to engender positive associations between the brand and the consumers they are trying to reach. The Internet of Things (IoT) applications, investments, and difficulties for organizations dealing with premium pricing also create a good quality perception among consumers (Henry, 2018). IoT has successfully made some of its product lines proprietary by charging premium pricing and limiting sales and manufacture. As a result, people begin to associate the word "luxury" with the things they buy. IoT applications, investments, and obstacles for organizations' products might be mitigated by charging premium rates (Henry, 2018). IoT applications, investments, and problems for organizations to maintain significantly high profitability and steady company growth are examples of how premium pricing strategies might be applied to various product lines (Henry, 2018).

Pricing Based on Value

Customer evaluation of value is the foundation of value-based pricing. It teaches you how to quantify intangible benefits as well as the importance of understanding demand elasticity and market competition.

Penetration Pricing

Companies adopt a penetrative pricing strategy for IoT applications because it generates more interest in their products and services through free trials and because it makes their products more accessible to a wider audience by lowering their price points (Baines, Fill, & Rosengren, 2017). This pricing model allows IoT commerce to enter a new market at a loss or with a very small profit margin.

Pricing based on Psychology

The use of psychological pricing has been useful (Henry, 2018) because there are so many distinct product categories and price points in the Internet of Things (IoT) applications, investments, and problems for organizations. The Internet of Things (IoT) applications, investments, and challenges for organizations also successfully increase the perceived worth of their products through the application of psychological pricing. Similarly, businesses can increase sales by using psychological pricing strategies when implementing Internet of Things (IoT) applications. The Internet of Things (IoT) Applications Investments and Challenges for Enterprises uses psychological pricing to encourage consumers to buy more of the product. Business investments in and challenges posed by IoT application development have the potential to reach a wider range of potential customers.

Geographical Pricing (Pricing Based on Location)

Using geographical pricing, businesses can more effectively break into new regional markets for IoT applications investments and problems (Henry, 2018). IoT applications, investments, and problems for businesses include the cost of shipping and any applicable customs duties for international orders. IoT applications, investments, and issues for businesses can be mitigated by geographical pricing by setting prices in each region according to the value of the local currency (Henry, 2018).

Prices Determined by Market Forces

IoT technology allows organizations to adopt an aggressive price strategy for currently available products. Market conditions and competitors' prices inform the pricing strategy. As part of this strategy, IoT commerce will attempt to match competitors' prices while also cutting costs to maximize profits. Businesses do better with competitive pricing as the cost curve continues to fall. Companies may now test out new platforms and price points thanks to technological advancements (Jennifer, 2022). This ensures that the goods may be purchased cheaply and conveniently. High rates of growth and experience are possible thanks to aggressive and competitive pricing strategies, which encourage consumers to form attachments to brands based on their products' features and benefits rather than their prices (Deepak & Jeyakumar, 2019). This, in turn, generates more brand equity and value for IoT for enterprises.

IoT for New Prices Introduction

The Internet of Things IoT applications, investments, and challenges for organizations guarantee to use introductory prices for newly released items. This indicates that the company's prices are more competitive than those of its rivals. Increased trial creation, deeper market penetration, and more brand awareness and recall are all possible thanks to the company's introductory pricing plan (Kucuk, 2017).

Bundles Pricing

Investments and Challenges for Enterprises is also well-known for its usage of a bundle pricing model for several product lines. Bundle pricing is used in the sales process for IoT applications, investments, and difficulties faced by businesses (Henry, 2018). Pricing in bundles encourages more customers to give a product a try. When compared to the cost of acquiring a new customer, the return on investment in IoT applications for businesses is much higher (Henry, 2018). Bundle pricing helps businesses manage costs and prices by reducing marketing and distribution expenditures associated with IoT applications, investments, and issues. IoT for businesses has additional value when packaged together under the banner of bundle pricing.

IoT and the Future of Pricing

Technology evolves and develops as the times do. To stay up with other technological developments, IoT will also continue to develop. According to experts, companies will be able to plan their expenditures for their whole use. Customers will be able to prepay for anticipated expenditures rather than pay for actual usage. Companies can save money in the long run by using this pricing technique to better predict and control their expenses.

Implications

This chapter looks at the application of IoT in the price and pricing of company products. Managers can select the following pricing strategy based on available evidence (High brand awareness and product innovation). High brand awareness-based pricing leads to market esteem for the IoT commerce, which means it may charge a premium over similar products sold by competitors. Product innovation is due to its cutting-edge capabilities, and this offering is seen as revolutionary in the current market. Modest premium pricing will not only draw attention to the product's features but also discourage new competitors from joining the market. New competitors can reduce profits if the premium price is too high. Managers can also enter into new markets *via* an IoT-based penetration pricing system.

CONCLUSION

This chapter looks at the application of IoT in the price and pricing of company products. Because of the Internet, information about prices and competitors can be disseminated quickly and openly, which may allow market forces to work more quickly and efficiently. Digital marketing is a notion made possible by the Internet, which allows businesses to have two-way conversations with their target audience. It removes barriers to information sharing based on geography and makes it possible to send communications with visual, auditory, and kinetic elements, as well as to facilitate two-way communication. Manufacturers can bypass the middleman and offer their wares and support services to consumers online. This effectively "disintermediates" the need for the middlemen of the past. Managers need to have a firm grasp on the concept of value, as well as its creation and expansion. Businesses can improve their customer satisfaction and economic utility thanks to the internet's many features. The IoT still has a lot of promise for commercial enterprises. Even if having a fantastic business idea is crucial at the outset of an organization's IoT plan, having a pricing and monetization strategy that customers can appreciate is even more important. Increased price transparency and its impact on differential pricing, commoditization and price pressure, dynamic pricing and auction, and alternative pricing methodologies are all ways in which the internet can affect the pricing strategy of a marketing campaign.

REFERENCES

Abratt, R., Bendixen, M. (2018). *Strategic marketing: Concepts and cases..* New York, United States: Routledge.
[http://dx.doi.org/10.4324/9780429489327]

Baines, P., Fill, C., Rosengren, S. (2017). *Marketing..* New York, United States: Oxford University Press.

Carniel, A. (2022). The ultimate guide to marketing mix: 4Ps, 7Ps, 8Ps, 4Cs, 7Cs. Available from: https://www.albertocarniel.com/post/marketing-mix.

Chui, M., Loffler, M., Roberts, R. (2010). *The internet of things.* McKinsey Global Institute.

Deepak, R., Jeyakumar, S. (2019). *Marketing management.* New Delhi, India: Educreation Publishing.

Dennis, C., Harris, , Sandhu, B. (2002). From bricks to clicks: understanding the e-consumer. *Qual. Mark. Res., 5*(4), 281-290.
[http://dx.doi.org/10.1108/13522750210443236]

Grewal, D., Levy, M. (2021). *M: marketing.* New York, United States: McGraw-Hill Education.

Groucutt, J., Hopkins, C. (2015). *Marketing.* London: Macmillan International Higher Education.

Henry, Z. (2018). Marketing Mix Of The Internet of Things IoT Applications investments and challenges for enterprises. Available from: https://www.case48.com/case/The-Internet-of-Things-IoT-Applica-ions-investments-and-challenges-for-enterprises-Marketing-Mix-19646.

Hoffman, D.L., Novak, T.P. (2018). Consumer and object experience in the Internet of Things: An assemblage theory approach. *J. Consum. Res., 44*(6), 1178-1204.
[http://dx.doi.org/10.1093/jcr/ucx105]

Jennifer, H. (June 1, 2022). Evolution of IoT Technology Pricing. Available from: https://www.link-labs.com/blog/evolution-of-iot-technology-pricing.

Kotabe, M., Helsen, K. (2020). *Global marketing management.*. Hoboken, New Jersey, United States: John Wiley & Sons.

Kotler, P., Keller, K. (2021). *Marketing Management (15th global edition).*. London, United Kingdom: Pearson Education Limited.

Kucuk, S. (2017). Marketing and Marketing Mix. *Visualizing Marketing.*. London, United Kingdom: Palgrave Macmillan.
[http://dx.doi.org/10.1007/978-3-319-48027-5_2]

Minerva, R. Biru, A. and Rotondi, D. (2015). Towards a definition of the Internet of Things (IoT). IEEE Technical Report, Revision 1, Published 27 May 2015.

Mittal, S. (2012). *Modern ICT for agricultural development and risk management in smallholder agriculture in India.*. CIMMYT.

Pogorelova, E.V., Yakhneeva, I.V., Agafonovaa, A.N., Prokubovskaya, A.O. (2016). Marketing Mix for E-commerce. *Int. J. Environ. Sci. Educ., 11*(14), 6744-6759.

Porter, M.E., Heppelmann, J.E. (2015). How smart, connected products are transforming companies. *Harv. Bus. Rev., 93*(10), 96-114.

Williams, T. (November 7, 2022). The Impact Of Internet Of Things (IOT) - In Marketing. Available from: https://www.theknowledgeacademy.com/blog/impact-of-internet-of-things-on-marketing-iot-in-marketing/.

CHAPTER 4

Promotion and the Internet of Things

Mohammed Majeed[1,*]**, Ibrahim Osman**[1] **and Abdul-Fatahi Abdul-Karim Abubakar**[1]

[1] *Marketing Department, Tamale Technical University, Tamale, Ghana*

Abstract: This chapter seeks to examine the potential effects of the Internet of Things (IoT) on the marketing and advertising strategies employed by firms to promote their products and services. The Internet of Things (IoT) has evolved as a novel paradigm for the future iteration of the Internet. The Internet of Things (IoT) involves the connection of a vast number of devices to the Internet, resulting in a significant data repository that can be utilized by a variety of applications. The future trajectory of the Internet is anticipated to involve the integration of diverse gadgets, establishing connections between physical items and digital elements, thereby expanding the boundaries of the global network. The Internet of Things (IoT) is a contemporary concept that pertains to items endowed with digital capabilities, enabling them to establish communication through the Internet. It is widely regarded as an integral component of the future Internet landscape.

Keywords: Advertising, Firm, Internet of things, Internet, Promotion, Technology.

INTRODUCTION

The advancement of technology has brought about changes in the methods used to communicate with consumers. The field of marketing has seen significant transformations in tandem with advancements in technology. The prevalence of Internet marketing is rapidly supplanting conventional approaches to marketing. The Internet of Things (IoT) is a novel paradigm shift within the field of technological innovation (IT), which pertains to the utilization of Internet connections for the purpose of transmitting and exchanging information. The Internet of Things (IoT) is an emerging paradigm that enables the interconnection of various objects *via* the Internet. These devices encompass sensors and actuators that possess the capability to function and transfer data with limited or no human interaction. The Internet of Things (IoT) has exerted a significant impact on various domains, with numerous applications having been successfully deployed

* **Corresponding author Mohammed Majeed:** Marketing Department, Tamale Technical University, Tamale, Ghana; E-mail: tunteya14june@gmail.com

Mohammed Majeed, Jonas Yomboi, Sulemana Ibrahim & Esther Asiedu (Eds.)

in sectors like healthcare, transportation, logistics, and manufacturing (Gubbi et al., 2013). Nevertheless, the advancement of the Internet of Things (IoT) is encountering numerous obstacles, particularly in the realm of data management (Pogorelova et al., 2016). New solutions may be necessary for managing IoT systems and services due to their unique properties, such as diverse enormous-scale designs and the presence of different and massive data. Conventional handling of information methodologies may become difficult to handle in this context. The Internet of Things (IoT) is predominantly facilitated by technological advancements that establish connections between gadgets, hence facilitating inter-device communication. Connectivity options encompass a variety of advantages and disadvantages, with certain alternatives being better suited for specific scenarios, such as intelligent houses, while others may be more fitting for Internet of Things (IoT) functions like automated manufacturing. The technologies can be classified into two distinct categories: IoT data protocols, which facilitate the exchange of information between devices in the absence of a web connection, and connected device protocols, which establish connections between devices and enable their integration with the internet. The promotional aspect within the marketing mix pertains to the Internet of Things. The investments and challenges associated with IoT devices for enterprises primarily pertain to the strategic approaches and initiatives undertaken by companies to enhance the visibility and marketability of their products and services. This encompasses various aspects such as brand promotion, product attributes, features, and overall business operations (Varadarajan, 2015; Gillespie & Swan, 2021). The primary focus of the communication pertains to investments and problems in Internet of Things (IoT) applications for organizations. Its intended audience consists of individuals or groups that the company aims to attract, with the objective of enhancing brand recognition, brand loyalty, and sales (Wu & Li, 2018; Grewal & Levy, 2021). Numerous academics have conducted research on the utilization of Internet-based technologies or platforms in the context of public relations endeavors (Dozier, Shen, Sweetser, & Barker, 2016; Tankosic, Ivetic, & Vucurevic, 2016; Wang, 2015). Additionally, certain scholars have employed descriptors such as Digital, Online, or E-Public Relations to characterize this emerging phenomenon (Vercic, Vercic, & Sriramesh, 2015). Nevertheless, there is a scarcity of scientific literature regarding the ramifications of the Internet of Things (IoT) on marketing promotion. The significance of the Internet of Things (IoT) in enhancing decision-making within the field of marketing research is of paramount importance. The implementation of Internet of Things (IoT) technologies holds the capacity to revolutionize the field of marketing research. According to Marek and Wozniczka (2017), it is of utmost importance to augment users' comprehension of the potential benefits that can be derived from utilizing Internet of Things (IoT) capabilities. The implementation of automated processes for generating real-time data flow facilitates marketing researchers in discerning efficacious ways to foster favorable client engagement. The increased availability of consumer data enhances the decision-making capabilities of both academics and practitioners, as it enables them to make more confident and well-informed decisions. The deployment of Internet of Things (IoT) solutions presents a multitude of opportunities for augmenting marketing research. This is particularly true for digital marketers who want access to extensive data regarding consumer trends and opinions related to the continuous utilization of Internet of Things (IoT) technologies. The availability of a larger dataset for analysis is perceived as beneficial for digital marketers, as it allows them to optimize certain procedures and effectively target varied consumer segments (Nguyen and Simkin, 2017). The clear prospect of doing predictive analysis on the needs and preferences of target customers arises from the direct linkage between the Internet of Things (IoT) and cloud computing. Hence, the chapter aims to look at the implications of IoTs on the promotion of a firm's products and services.

LITERATURE

IoT

Fletcher (2015) provides a comprehensive historical context for the Internet of Things (IoT) by tracing its inception back to the foundation of the MIT Auto-ID Centre in 1999. The establishment of the Centre aimed to develop a diverse range of detection methods suitable for industrial applications, with the objective of minimizing errors, facilitating automated processes, and improving overall efficiency. One crucial element of the technology in question was the utilization of Radio Frequency Identification (RFID) tags. These tags facilitated the detection, distinctive verification, and provision of detailed information regarding the objects being tagged by centrally located services. Subsequent efforts yielded advancements in the capability to trace objects throughout the entire production and distribution process, discern manufacturing obstacles, minimize reliance on human labor, and mitigate instances of theft. The author notes that the progress of IoT is propelled by the advancements in technology for wireless communication and computers embedded in devices. The Internet of Things (IoT) endeavors to establish interconnectedness across several facets of human existence, wherein intelligent devices would furnish notifications, dispense guidance, and deliver computerized aid. Despite the significant growth in the advancement of technology and the increasing uses of the Internet of Things (IoT), there exists a considerable degree of diversity and ambiguity in its definition. Minerva *et al.* (2015) present a comprehensive and universally accepted characterization of the Internet of Things (IoT), offering a precise and unambiguous delineation. The concept of the Internet of Things (IoT) entails the creation of a network that is self-configuring, responsive, and intricate, connecting various objects to the Internet by utilizing universally accepted communication protocols. The entities that are networked possess either a physical or virtual manifestation within the digital realm. They possess the ability to sense and actuate, as well as a programming capabilities aspect, and are distinguishable by unique identification. The concept of the Internet of Things (IoT) pertains to the integration of sensors and actuators within tangible things, enabling their communication with IT infrastructure through wired or wireless networks. This interconnectedness facilitates the digital monitoring and potential control of the physical realm.

Promotion

Marketing, applications, and events (both online and off) are all part of promotion (Carniel, 2022). It changes depending on the target audience and the marketing approach taken. Advertising, sales force, marketing by mail, PR, advertising expenditures, *etc.*, are all factors that must be considered when promoting a product or service. Promotion exists to increase brand recognition and demand for a company's goods and services. It is useful for getting people to pick your goods over the competition. The following are examples of promotional activities: Commercial messages promoting goods and services that are paid for but not delivered personally are what we call advertising. In public relations, one must manage and direct the content and quantity of information that is disseminated about their organization to the public and other entities. The goal of every successful marketing plan is to increase sales by reaching out to potential customers. Promotion extends to online elements like the design and style of a company's webpage or the content provided on social media handles like Twitter and Instagram, as well as offline elements like word-of-mouth recommendations and physical storefronts.

In order to better engage with and communicate with the client, the promotion mix of the marketing mix can be further subdivided into various messaging channels. Everything in marketing culminates at the instant a buyer experiences the advertised benefit. The goal of any marketing campaign is met when the intended audience receives and responds to the advertised offer.

A marketer can use the promotion mix's strategies to accomplish a variety of marketing goals, such as raising brand awareness or launching a new product. However, in addition to the news, music, work, chores, family, and friends, consumers also have to deal with a constant stream of marketing messages. The modern customer is notoriously hard to get a hold of due to everyone's hectic schedules. If you want to reach today's harried consumers, you need more than just one channel of communication. In order to make a meaningful connection with the client and achieve the communication goal, marketers must integrate numerous communication elements.

Promotion Internet of Things (PmIoTs)

The advertising approach for investment and problems related to the Internet of Things (IoT) applications in organizations also lays significant emphasis on the utilization of promotional methods and approaches. Promotional strategies facilitate the engagement of firms with customers and exert a direct impact on them in the context of investments and problems pertaining to the Internet of Things (IoT) applications. The promotion activities of firms who invest in Internet of Things (IoT) applications utilize a comprehensive approach, encompassing all aspects of the IoT ecosystem. Promotion in the electronic environment is characterized by a wide range of tools and features. According to Pogorelova *et al.* (2016), promotion activities facilitate customer engagement in a communication process, hence motivating people to undertake specific actions such as approval, registration, download, purchase, and referral. Furthermore, in the event of a successful marketing campaign, the distribution of information pertaining to the company, its product, and its service takes on a viral characteristic, resulting in a level of exposure that rivals that of prominent media personalities. The growth of commercial indicators is also influenced by the heightened curiosity of the audience (Yakhneeva & Podolyak, 2009). The utilization of data created by the Internet of Things (IoT) enables organizations to tailor campaigns to individual customers, fostering a perception of attentiveness and engagement from the firm (iCulture, 2016). The latest Bluetooth smart technology is employed, which is compatible with all prominent mobile platforms. By disseminating data to all suitable devices within proximity, mobile phones are capable of receiving information pertaining to products that align with the preferences of the phone's user. This technology provides users with access to a range of features, including photos, videos, reviews, tailored pricing, and social media updates. The level of detail is sufficiently high enough that the client can be guided through a narrative and provided with information about the product that is most relevant to them, so significantly increasing their in-store experience. There exists a potential for marketers operating in the realm of promotion to enhance customer brand interaction and create tailored campaigns. However, excessive inclusion of extremely detailed personal information in ads may potentially undermine the confidence of customers, leading to a decreased willingness to engage with the product.

Banner advertisements are a form of online advertising that involves the display of graphical ads on websites. A banner refers to a visual representation shown on a webpage with the primary purpose of advertising. Banner advertising is widely regarded as the prevailing form of advertising utilized on the Internet. Fagerstron and Ghinea (2011) conducted a study. Banner advertisements are commonly found as compact message strips strategically positioned in prominent sections of regularly accessed websites. According to Heiligtag and Xu (2006), banner advertisements function similarly to placement advertisements found in traditional print media. In order to attract the attention of viewers, banner advertisements currently include animation, Java programming, and multimedia elements. Banner advertisements serve a valuable purpose in generating product awareness and effectively conveying pertinent information about these products. According to Kleindle and Burrow (2005), customers should not experience feelings of intimidation or surveillance due to the extent of personal information disclosed through personalized advertising campaigns when corporations engage in customer targeting. The Internet of Things (IoT) enables marketers to effectively target customers and improve their overall experience. However, this also presents a difficulty for marketers in finding a balance between utilizing sensitive information for targeting purposes and addressing privacy issues.

In the realm of personal selling, the role traditionally fulfilled by a seller or consultant is progressively being supplanted by intelligent bots. E-commerce bots facilitate the purchase of various commodities. Banking bots are capable of delivering a range of financial services.

Sales promotion encompasses several strategies, such as social media calls to action, e-mail marketing, web conferences, and webinars. Social networks are extensively utilized to enhance customer loyalty, encourage their active involvement in sales promotion activities, and facilitate the dissemination of marketing information among their social connections.

Public relations is executed through the utilization of social media marketing, content marketing, and referral marketing strategies. Consumers who assume the role of "brand advocates" play a crucial role in fostering public relations, mitigating unfavorable perceptions, and bolstering the company's reputation among the intended demographic. According to Nielsen's (2015) survey, individuals across several age groups, including Generation Z, Millennials, Generation X, Baby Boomers, and the Silent Generation, exhibit the highest level of trust in advertising formats when it comes to recommendations from friends. The digital landscape enables consumers to actively participate in a communication process with a brand, as well as with all relevant target audiences that the organization aims to engage.

One of the tools employed to facilitate promotional efforts is search engine marketing, which serves to guarantee search engine indexing, achieve a prominent position in search results, and enhance organic traffic.

Contextual Segmentation

The proliferation of Internet of Things (IoT) devices among users has facilitated the collection and analysis of data pertaining to their purchasing habits. Consequently, this has opened up avenues for employing contextually tailored advertising techniques to directly engage with these users (Borrás, 2022). Contextual advertising is currently implemented through numerous platforms, such as Google Search Ads. When users engage in searches on their mobile devices, they are presented with the most pertinent advertisements based on their current location.

Community Influencers

Enterprises utilize local influencers as a means of on-ground promotional activities for their investments and issues in the applications of the Internet of Things (IoT). The investments and problems associated with Internet of Things (IoT) applications in organizations involve the identification of individuals who possess strong and confident qualities to serve as brand ambassadors within the communities they represent. Enterprises invest in applications of the Internet of Things (IoT) and face many problems. These obstacles are addressed by providing spokespersons and members of the community with a choice of products. They are then invited to personally experience the benefits of using these products.

In-Store Advertising

Real-time marketing in stores is another way the Internet of Things can be utilized to boost business (Borrás, 2022). Beacons are the foundational technology for this application. Beacons are tiny transmitters that broadcast Bluetooth signals to adjacent devices. This allows them to track a customer's cart as they move through the checkout procedure and provide recommendations based on the items the user has brought. The store's income and AOV both rise as a result of these factors.

Reward Programs

Often known as loyalty programs, these are marketing strategies implemented by businesses to encourage customer loyalty and repeat purchases. These programs typically

The organization responsible for commitments and problems in Internet of Things (IoT) applications has implemented loyalty card program for its client base. The loyalty card facilitates the redemption of accumulated points by consumers, enabling them to acquire items or other enticing presents as determined by the company. AI-powered personalization engines have emerged as a highly efficacious method for facilitating productive marketing endeavors in contemporary times.

Location-Based Advertising

Internet of Things (IoT) devices are equipped with Global Positioning System (GPS) technology, which facilitates the monitoring and tracing of individuals or items' whereabouts. The aforementioned study conducted by Borrás (2022) suggests that this data can be utilized by advertisers to enhance the delivery of more pertinent advertisements, akin to the Google search ads stated before. A potential utilization of this technology involves the display of advertisements to those in close proximity to a brick-and-mortar establishment. Rather than deploying beacons within the confines of a store, advertisers have the option to position them externally, enabling individuals who are in close proximity to get customized ads on their mobile devices. As an illustration, a dining establishment has the capability to transmit communication regarding exclusive culinary selections available for the given day.

Internet/Digital Marketing

Internet and digital marketing encompasses the use of various technologies to engage consumers at various touchpoints. Many channels are available to marketers to communicate with consumers and build product identities. Websites, web pages, user profiles, elements, and customer relationship management (CRM) platforms are all examples of tools that can be used. The various online resources are coordinated to increase customer interest in and visits to branded sites. The focus of Internet marketing is on direct interaction with a targeted audience. Consider digital marketing to be the engine that instantly connects you with your target audience and solicits their instantaneous input. Digital marketing makes use of the Internet, which includes web pages, digital advertisements, and digital platforms for two-way communication. Mobile technology, such as SMS and mobile apps, is another type of digital marketing.

Personalization Engines

Personalization engines integrate several types of first-party data, including demographic information, sales data, support call records, and consumer activity data. This facilitates advertisers in gaining a deeper comprehension of individual customers and constructing comprehensive client databases. Additionally, it empowers firms to effectively interact with customers by delivering pertinent material during critical moments (Donlan, 2023).

Public Relations

The Internet of Things (IoT) presents significant prospects for the field of public relations to extract and analyze data pertaining to relevant target audiences. Additionally, it would be beneficial to actively utilize the acquired knowledge in order to make well-informed decisions pertaining to the anticipation and fulfillment of the diverse requirements of different stakeholders. The Internet of Things (IoT) presents significant prospects for the field of public relations to extract and analyze data pertaining to relevant target audiences. Additionally, it would be beneficial to actively utilize the acquired knowledge in order to make well-informed judgments regarding the anticipation and fulfillment of the diverse requirements of different publics (Usaini et al., 2018).

At present, there exists a range of publicity software solutions that facilitate the extraction of online dialogues, monitoring of market trends, engagement with influencers, and tracking of rivals' activities for enterprises. There are more software packages available that facilitate the identification of journalists based on their specific areas of coverage and geographical locations. These applications also provide alert services for tracking online references. However, a significant portion of software systems continue to prioritize communication with journalists and editors rather than establishing direct connections with the intended audience. The act of distributing internet publications to journalists necessitates that they assume the responsibility of vetting the content, as not all received materials may be suitable for publication. One significant drawback of the software is its deficiency in interconnectivity, which hampers the ability to retrieve multiple channels of data from various sources.

Personalized Emails

The use of tailored email communication with clients has the potential to enhance both the rate of opening and click-through rates. This objective can be accomplished by employing personalized strategies such as acknowledging the recipient by their name, leveraging their previous spending or browsing behavior to recommend relevant products, and customizing the contents of the email to align with their specific interests (Donlan, 2023).

Intent-Based Advertising

Intent-based advertisement is a marketing approach that involves the segmentation of consumers based on their motivations or thoughts toward a particular brand. This facilitates the enhancement of company tactics to get more favorable outcomes. Internet of Things (IoT) devices gather data pertaining to the intentions of users. According to Borrás (2022), brands have the ability to utilize this data in order to subtly influence consumers towards making a purchase. For instance, when an individual visits an electronics retail establishment with the explicit purpose of purchasing speakers, it is possible to present them with advertisements that are directly associated with speakers or supplementary merchandise.

Dynamic Website Content

The utilization of many data points, including geographical information, browsing patterns, and previous transactions, to tailor website content has been shown to enhance customer satisfaction and foster greater user involvement (Donlan,2023). An instance of this might involve the presentation of customized overlays, linked information, or banners on a company's website, which would showcase recommended goods or exhibit local events or promotions, all contingent upon the geographical location of the user.

CRM Ads

CRM advertisements enable marketers to establish connections between CRM contacts and their profiles on various networks, like Facebook and Google. This facilitates the creation of tailored target segments. According to Donlan (2023), the utilization of an advanced customer interaction platform enables the dynamic creation of client segments, which can be tailored depending on consumer habits and updated in actual time.

Personalized Advertisements with Beacons

Beacons are wireless gadgets capable of transmitting a constant stream of data and signals to other intelligent devices. The integration of Internet of Things (IoT) technology has facilitated collaboration with beacons, which have historically served as essential components in GPS navigation systems and radio stations. According to Zhao (2023), marketing aides play a significant role in the development of extremely effective tailored commercials. Beacons have the potential to assist advertisers in generating precise in-store marketing. Interior indicators, when utilized in conjunction with beacons, possess the capability to discern the specific purchases made by consumers within supermarket or shopping mall environments. Subsequently, Bluetooth connectivity is employed to establish connections with proximate smart devices, such as patrons' smartphones, facilitating the transmission of tailored adverts or coupons. For example, in the event that a consumer is in the process of inspecting their milk and happens to come across an advertisement for bread either on their mobile device or on a screen located near the checkout counter, they may become aware of their need to purchase bread as well. In addition to facilitating in-store advertising, beacons and IoT technologies can also offer advantages in the realm of location-based and contextual-targeted advertisements. The technologies employed in this context aim to tailor these advertisements to enhance their efficacy in addressing the immediate demands of customers.

Interactive Advertising

According to Park (2020), advertising is believed by certain individuals to facilitate the acquisition and retention of brand knowledge and the associated advantages through message repetition and the establishment of connections between companies, logos, visuals, and benefits. This process can be understood as a manifestation of classical conditioning. The advent of the Internet of Things has transformed the nature of communication between brands and users, rendering it no longer unidirectional (Borrás, 2022). Through the implementation of an effective marketing campaign, consumers have the potential to proactively seek additional information regarding a product. This can be facilitated by utilizing Quick Response (QR) codes, among other strategies.

Print

Newspapers and periodicals serve as platforms for the dissemination of print media and advertisements. These forms of media are commonly consumed by a wide range of individuals, including the target audience of the Internet of Things IoT utilization, stakes and, obstacles for companies (Chernev, 2018; Iacobucci, 2021; Stead & Hastings, 2018).

Unveiling Consumer Intentions

Comprehending the motivations of consumers is a crucial undertaking for organizations as it enables them to forecast the future market potential of a product. Devices that are connected to the Internet of Things (IoT) network serve as effective instruments for gathering customer data, including personal interests and routines. Based on this data, marketers have the ability to construct a comprehensive database that is specifically tailored towards identifying potential consumers, doing in-depth analysis of their behavioral patterns, and generating precise predictions. In this manner, brands possess the ability to not only formulate marketing and advertising strategies but also enhance product designs by leveraging insights into consumers' interests and requirements. Intent marketing can also serve as a means to produce customized advertising campaigns and propose future trajectories for the brand's advancement. The integration of IoT technologies and mobile applications is consistently seen as a very synergistic partnership. According to Zhao (2023), the Internet of Things (IoT) technology enables mobile applications to capture and analyze users' behavioral patterns during app usage, afterward storing this customer data in a cloud-based database.

Sales Promotion

Sales promotion refers to a comprehensive range of predominantly temporary incentives that are strategically developed to encourage consumers or the trade to make quick and/or larger purchases of a product. This is achieved through price reductions or the inclusion of additional value. Within this chapter, the concept of sales promotion will be elucidated as the collection of incentives aimed at stimulating consumers to engage in the purchase of a product or service through the use of the Internet.

Radio

The term "radio" refers to a form of wireless communication that utilizes electromagnetic waves to transmit. Enterprises invest in and face issues related to the applications of the Internet of Things (IoT). Additionally, they utilize radio commercials as a means to attract a certain portion of the target market. Radio communications pertaining to investments and problems for organizations in the context of Internet of Things (IoT) applications are typically characterized by brevity and a primary emphasis on functional appeal (Išoraitė, 2016; Groucutt & Hopkins, 2015).

Personal Selling

Personal selling is a marketing strategy that involves direct communication between a salesperson and a potential customer. It is a form of persuasive communication. Personal selling is a method of communication when an individual imparts information with the intention of persuading a potential consumer to make a purchase, whether it be a product, service, concept, or any other offering. Personal selling involves the utilization of Internet of Things (IoT) enabled technology and verbal communication to facilitate interactions between a salesperson or sales team and one or more potential buyers. The primary goal of personal selling is to either secure a sale or exert influence over the purchasing decision. In this chapter, the researchers provide a definition of personal selling as a form of direct presentation or communication between a salesperson and targeted consumers facilitated through the use of the Internet.

The Role of Email Marketing in IoT Commerce

Email marketing is a direct marketing strategy that IoT commerce can employ to establish direct communication with its prospective clients. Email marketing has the potential to assist IoT commerce in effectively targeting prospects with a high likelihood of conversion. This is achieved through the utilization of data obtained by the firm from its kiosks, trade marketing efforts, and customer surveys.

SEO

Search engine marketing (SEM) refers to the practice of promoting websites and increasing their visibility in search engine results pages (SERPs) through paid advertising. SEM involves various techniques. Search engine marketing (SEM) has become a prevalent advertising medium in recent years. This approach involves displaying advertisements to customers in accordance with their search and browsing history. Similar to email advertising, this approach can lead to the delivery of targeted advertisements to potential buyers who have a high likelihood of being interested in the products and actively seeking information about them.

Direct Marketing

Direct marketing refers to a promotional strategy that involves communicating directly with potential customers to promote products or services. This approach typically bypasses intermediatly. Enterprises utilize direct marketing to promote and distribute their specialized products and offers inside the realm of Internet of Things (IoT) applications. This approach involves targeted communication and promotional strategies to reach potential customers while also addressing the investments and issues associated with IoT implementation. Enterprises utilize the Internet of Things (IoT) applications to invest in and address difficulties. One such approach involves directly reaching out to potential clients, particularly those in the business-to-business (B2B) sector, *via* email. The purpose of these communications is to provide comprehensive information regarding the enterprise's product offerings and features. Organizations are investing in applications of the Internet of Things (IoT) to enhance their operations. These applications utilize personalized messages to attract and engage new clients and consumers, thereby expanding their business. However, organizations also face some problems when implementing IoT applications. In addition to utilizing direct emailing, firms involved in the Internet of Things (IoT) applications also employ telemarketing and direct mail as means of targeting audiences through direct marketing (Chernev, 2018; Sahaf, 2019).

The Facilitation of Public Relations Communication

The Internet functions as the primary means of communication for numerous organizations. Public relations specialists have the ability to promptly disseminate firm news and advancements in product innovation to the general public and consumers. According to Frenz (2023), websites facilitate interactive connections between public relations representatives and consumers. Email facilitates efficient communication between public relations experts and media representatives, enabling streamlined dissemination of mass press releases to announce significant corporate developments.

The phenomenon of Increasingly Discerning Consumers

The advent of the Internet has resulted in the emergence of increasingly discerning consumers, who now possess the ability to communicate their discontent to a vast audience. Technologically adept consumers leverage the Internet as a means to conduct thorough research and enhance their knowledge of products prior to making a purchase. Consumer discontent is frequently caused by insufficient or inaccurate information (Frenz, 2023). In addition to their primary expectations, a significant number of consumers also anticipate individualized interactions from customer support services, as well as the ability to customize products according to their preferences.

IMC

Integrated marketing communications (IMC) refers to the strategic coordination and integration of various marketing communication tools and tactics inside an organization. IMC aims to ensure that all marketing messages are appropriately sent to the right audience. The advertisement and promotional messages of the Internet of Things (IoT) applications, investments, and challenges for enterprises are strategically developed to align with an integrated plan. This approach ensures that the messages and communication conveyed through various mediums and channels are consistent with the overall campaign, thereby minimizing confusion and discrepancies (Gillespie & Swan, 2021; Kotler & Keller, 2021). The utilization of integrated marketing and integrated media has facilitated enterprises in establishing robust relationships with consumers by directly engaging them in conversations and discussions (Deepak & Jeyakumar, 2019; Sahaf, 2019; Stead & Hastings, 2018). This has been made possible through investments and challenges associated with the Internet of Things (IoT) applications.

The Complexity of the Media Mix

Prior to the widespread adoption of the Internet, public relations professionals employed a more straightforward combination of media channels to facilitate the promotion of organizations and products. The previous forms of media amalgamation encompassed magazines, newspapers, billboards, television, and radio. The contemporary media mix incorporates traditional components alongside modern aspects such as email, websites, blogs, viral videos, and webcasts (Frenz, 2023). In order to maintain a favorable public perception, it is imperative for public relations specialists to exercise control over each of these emerging components. In addition to PR professionals, other stakeholders, including members of the public and competing companies, possess the ability to generate and manipulate numerous new media components. Consequently, it becomes imperative for PR professionals to engage in continuous monitoring of online platforms in order to mitigate the potential impact of adverse online publicity.

Enables the Promotion of Products or Services

The term "IoT" can be identified as an emerging element within the domains of business analytics and digital marketing. Organizations have the potential to provide a novel product or service by leveraging consumer market segmentation. According to Pauget and Dammak (2019), this particular attribute can serve as a fundamental basis for the implementation of customer-centric marketing strategies. According to Moradi and Badrinarayanan (2021), Internet of Things (IoT) devices have the potential to reduce the inconvenience associated with the advertisement process. These technologies offer the target audience the ability to obtain product or brand-related information in a manner that aligns with their own choices and preferences.

The Topic of Discussion Pertains to In-Store Promotions

The investments and problems associated with Internet of Things (IoT) applications in companies also encompass the utilization of in-store promotions to attract customers, enhance sales, and elevate brand recognition and reputation for the products or services being offered (Baines, Fill, & Rosengren, 2017). In the context of enterprise investments and problems in the realm of the Internet of Things (IoT) applications, in-store promotions encompass various strategies, such as providing price reductions, loyalty points, and flash sales for their items. Furthermore, the organization additionally allocates resources toward enhancing the point-of-sale (POS) systems within its physical retail establishments (Stead & Hastings, 2018; Groucutt & Hopkins, 2015).

Enhancing Consumer Awareness with Transparent Product Information

A further application of Internet of Things (IoT) technology within the realm of advertising involves the provision of comprehensive product information to customers, hence augmenting the level of engagement between consumers and sales personnel. QR codes provide a means of achieving this objective. QR codes are ubiquitously present in various consumer-oriented contexts, including product packaging, restaurant menus, and promotional materials. QR codes are a type of two-dimensional barcode, sometimes referred to as Quick Response codes, because of their rapid readability and capacity for storing substantial amounts of information (Zhao, 2023). QR codes are barcodes that can be scanned by machines. Devices equipped with a camera, such as smartphones, have the capability to identify and read the label. In the realm of advertising, QR codes offer a more convenient means for consumers to reach a brand's website and obtain product information. This is achieved by utilizing their cellphones to scan the code, eliminating the need to manually input keywords or URL connections. In addition, QR codes are frequently employed by advertising as a means to endorse particular incentives, such as coupons or discounts.

Conventional Advertising

The concept of conventional advertising refers to the traditional methods and practices employed by businesses and organizations to promote their products or services. Enterprises persist in employing conventional marketing methods and promotional channels alongside their investments and challenges in the Internet of Things (IoT) applications, primarily for the goal of mass marketing. The corporation places particular emphasis on television advertisements and print media advertising (Išoraitė, 2016; Iacobucci, 2021).

The Advantages of Websites

An effectively managed and visually appealing corporate website has the potential to counterbalance adverse online publicity arising from dissatisfied consumers or disgruntled staff members. Public relations practitioners often utilize the company's official website as a means of engaging with many stakeholders, including the general public, consumers, and representatives from other media organizations (Frenz, 2023). Websites serve as a platform for introducing businesses or products, offering a comprehensive range of information and product customization options that align with the expectations of contemporary consumers. Public relations personnel have the capability to effectively handle various components of the new media mix by incorporating them into the webpages of a company's official website.

Social Media

Social media platforms are used for the purpose of marketing and promoting products, services, or brands. Social media marketing has emerged as a prominent modern strategy for organizations to promote and advertise their investments and address the issues associated with the Internet of Things (IoT) applications. The organization has a formal presence and profiles on various social media platforms, including Facebook and Instagram. These channels are consistently utilized by the corporation to advertise its offers as well as highlight the qualities and attributes of its products (Stead & Hastings, 2018). Moreover, corporations utilize these platforms to communicate with consumers regarding the utilization of specials and discounts, hence enhancing in-store foot traffic. This is particularly relevant for the Internet of Things (IoT) applications, which face investments and obstacles in their implementation.

Television (TV)

Television advertising is typically scheduled during prime time to maximize their visibility and audience reach. This strategic placement is influenced by the investments and challenges faced by organizations in the Internet of Things (IoT) applications. Television advertising employs both functional and emotional appeals to effectively convey the message of investments and problems in the Internet of Things (IoT) applications for organizations to their target audiences (Iacobucci, 2021; Stead & Hastings, 2018).

Implications

It is required that both academics and practitioners should take into account the perspectives of consumers regarding Internet of Things (IoT) solutions. This practice is valuable in the development of a reliable knowledge base within the domain. Consumer perspectives have been identified as encompassing a comprehensive and multifaceted nature. The primary characteristics encompassing user experience in relation to Internet of Things (IoT) solutions encompass behavioral, emotive, sensory, intellectual, and social aspects. The integration of these elements yields crucial understandings regarding the specific cognitive state of customers, empowering scholars and professionals to devise efficacious Internet of Things (IoT) solutions that are adaptable across various scenarios. The manner in which customers respond to the implementation of particular Internet of Things (IoT) tools enables information technology (IT) professionals to develop tailored solutions that effectively cater to consumer requirements and anticipations. Consumers exhibit a propensity to establish connections across several dimensions of the Internet of Things (IoT), namely through textual, visual, and auditory means. Consequently, the content that has been generated can be effectively examined in order to reveal distinct network configurations. Future research should prioritize enhancing the collaboration between academics and practitioners in order to generate more definitive findings regarding the strategic trajectory for the advancement of transparent and complete Internet of Things (IoT) solutions.

CONCLUSION

The present study investigated the utilization of Internet of Things (IoT) technology in the field of marketing research. The advent of IoT solutions has presented marketers with unique capabilities that enable them to transform conventional marketing research practices and substitute them with more extensive and precise types of data analysis. The utilization of Internet of Things (IoT) devices has been demonstrated to have a positive impact on the improvement of information exchange within the field of marketing research. The advent of Internet of Things (IoT) technology has provided digital marketing experts with a diverse array of tools and techniques, allowing them to enhance their research efforts and introduce novel perspectives to the field of marketing. Promotion encompasses a range of tactics, such as display and paid search advertising, mobile advertising, and social media marketing. The utilization of these tools is intended to engage customers in the communication and promotional process, facilitating the dissemination of brand messaging.

REFERENCES

Baines, P., Fill, C., Rosengren, S. (2017). *Marketing.* New York, United States: Oxford University Press.

Borrás, H. (2022). Benefits of IoT in Advertising. Available from: https://www.cyberclick.net/numericalblogen/benefits-of-iot-in-advertising#:~:text=IoT%20devices%20have%20GPS%20that,people%20near%20a%20physical%20store.

Chernev, A. (2018). *Strategic marketing management..* Berlin/Heidelberg, Germany: Cerebellum Press.

Carniel, A. (2022). The ultimate guide to marketing mix: 4Ps, 7Ps, 8Ps, 4Cs, 7Cs. Available from: https://www.albertocarniel.com/post/marketing-mix.

Deepak, R., Jeyakumar, S. (2019). *Marketing management..* New Delhi, India: Educreation Publishing.

Dozier, D.M., Shen, H., Sweetser, K.D., Barker, V. (2016). Demographics and Internet behaviors as predictors of active publics. *Public Relat. Rev., 42*(1), 82-90.
[http://dx.doi.org/10.1016/j.pubrev.2015.11.006]

Donlan, K. (2023). Understanding the 4 Ps of Marketing through Digital Transformation. Available from: https://emarsys.com/learn/blog/4-ps-of-marketing-importance/.

Frenz, R. (2023). The Positive & Negative Effects of Technological PR. Available from: https://smallbusiness.chron.com/positive-negative-effects-technological-pr-20928.html.

Fagerstrøm, A., Ghinea, G. (2011). On the motivating impact of price and online recommendations at the point of online purchase. *Int. J. Inf. Manage., 31*(2), 103-110.
[http://dx.doi.org/10.1016/j.ijinfomgt.2010.10.013]

Gubbi, J., Buyya, R., Marusic, S., Palaniswami, M. (2013). Internet of Things (IoT): A vision, architectural elements, and future directions. *Future Gener. Comput. Syst., 29*(7), 1645-1660. [September.]. [http://dx.doi.org/10.1016/j.future.2013.01.010]

Gillespie, K., Swan, K. (2021). *Global marketing.* New York, United States: Routledge. [http://dx.doi.org/10.4324/9781003141709]

Grewal, D., Levy, M. (2021). *M: marketing.* New York, United States: McGraw-Hill Education.

Groucutt, J., Hopkins, C. (2015). *Marketing.* London: Macmillan International Higher Education.

Kotler, P., Keller, K. (2021). *Marketing Management (15th global edition).* London, United Kingdom: Pearson Education Limited.

Minerva, R. Biru, A. and Rotondi, D. (2015). Towards a definition of the Internet of Things (IoT). IEEE Technical Report, Revision 1, Published 27 May 2015.

Moradi, M., Badrinarayanan, V. (2021). The effects of brand prominence and narrative features on crowdfunding success for entrepreneurial aftermarket enterprises. *J. Bus. Res., 124*, 286-298. [http://dx.doi.org/10.1016/j.jbusres.2020.12.002]

Park, S. (2020). Marketing management (Vol. 3). Retrieved June 2022, Available from: https://books.google.com.pk/books/about/Marketing_Management.html?id=p6v7DwAAQBAJ&redir_esc=y.

Pogorelova, E.V., Yakhneeva, I.V., Agafonovaa, A.N., Prokubovskaya, A.O. (2016). Marketing Mix for E-commerce. *Int. J. Environ. Sci. Educ., 11*(14), 6744-6759.

Pauget, B., Dammak, A. (2019). The implementation of the Internet of Things: What impact on organizations? *Technol. Forecast. Soc. Change, 140*, 140-146. [http://dx.doi.org/10.1016/j.techfore.2018.03.012]

Sahaf, A. (2019). *Strategic marketing: Making decisions for strategic advantage..* New Delhi, India: PHI Learning Pvt. Ltd..

Stead, M., Hastings, G. (2018). Advertising in the social marketing mix: getting the balance right. *Social Marketing.* (pp. 29-43). London, England: Psychology Press. [http://dx.doi.org/10.4324/9781315805795-3]

Tankosic, M., Ivetic, P., Vucurevic, V. (2016). Features of interactive public relations: Using web 2.0 to establish a two-way communication with the consumers. *International Journal of Economic and Management Systems, 1*, 290-295.

Usaini, S., Nelson, O., Bamgboye, O., Amodu, L., Afolabi, F., Evaristus, A. (2018). Internet, social media and computer-mediated relationship among engineering undergraduate students. *International Journal of Civil Engineering and Technology, 9*(13), 1651-1657.

Varadarajan, R. (2015). Strategic marketing, marketing strategy and market strategy. *AMS Rev., 5*(3-4), 78-90. [http://dx.doi.org/10.1007/s13162-015-0073-9]

Verčič, D., Verčič, A.T., Sriramesh, K. (2015). Looking for digital in public relations. *Public Relat. Rev., 41*(2), 142-152. [http://dx.doi.org/10.1016/j.pubrev.2014.12.002]

Wang, Y. (2015). Incorporating social media in public relations: A synthesis of social media-related public relations research. *Public Relat. J., 9*(3), 1-14.

Wu, Y.L., Li, E.Y. (2018). Marketing mix, customer value, and customer loyalty in social commerce. *Internet Res., 28*(1), 74-104. [http://dx.doi.org/10.1108/IntR-08-2016-0250]

Zhao, Y. (2023). 3 Ways IoT Benefits Advertising. Available from: https://www.aitimejournal.com/how-io--benefits-advertising/.

CHAPTER 5

Internet of Things and Marketing Mix

Mohammed Majeed[1,*]

[1] *Department of Marketing, Tamale Technical University, Tamale, Ghana*

Abstract: A genuine innovation for companies is the Internet of Things. Contemporary business sectors can be totally transformed by tiny gadgets with strong algorithms at their core, which can lower costs, boost productivity, and eliminate dangers. This chapter's goal is to review the body of research on the connection between the Internet of Things and the marketing mix. Today's businesses have access to a multitude of instruments and platforms that have improved our ability to communicate with clients (promotion) and link them with the goods and services (place), price, products, people, and physicals that will improve their lives. The success of our campaigns is still, nonetheless, firmly rooted in the four fundamental marketing tenets of product, pricing, place, and promotion. Effective marketers have the ability to combine these concepts with strategies like the ones listed above to get the consistent, lucrative results that their companies require.

Keywords: Internet of things, Marketing mix, Product, Price, Promotion, Place.

INTRODUCTION

In the contemporary corporate environment characterized by intense competition and reliance on technology, the mere presence of a website or participation in conventional marketing practices falls short of meeting the necessary requirements. The Internet of Things (IoT) is undergoing a rapid transformation of the global landscape and holds significant promise for providing advantages to organizations across several sectors. The proliferation of interconnected gadgets has significant ramifications for marketers seeking to engage their target audiences. The Internet of Things (IoT) refers to the interconnectedness of both electronic and physical components (Darius, 2023). This connectivity facilitates interoperability across commonplace objects, such as appliances and bells for doors, and *via* the World Wide Web. By leveraging sensors and integrated processors, these interconnected devices possess the capability to be controlled from a distance, enabling them to engage with their surroundings and exchange

---

[*] **Corresponding author Mohammed Majeed:** Department of Marketing, Tamale Technical University, Tamale, Ghana; E-mail: tunteya14june@gmail.com

data autonomously without the need for human intervention. The 4p model of marketing encompasses the fundamental components of product, price, promotion, and place, as discussed by Chernev (2018) and Kucuk (2017). The marketing mix is a widely recognized term used to describe the model. The marketing mix of The Internet of Things (IoT) encompasses various applications, investments, and problems for organizations. This framework enables enterprises to effectively achieve their marketing objectives and exert a positive influence on their target audience (Baines, Fill, & Rosengren, 2017). The marketing mix elements are commonly employed by firms in the Internet of Things (IoT) applications to promote their products and services, as well as to facilitate brand development and building endeavors. The development and implementation of marketing plans and strategies are of utmost importance for enterprises, particularly in relation to the Internet of Things (IoT) applications. This is essential for the purpose of establishing and maintaining a competitive advantage (Chernev, 2018; Stead & Hastings, 2018; Grewal & Levy, 2021). The investments and problems associated with the applications of the Internet of Things (IoT) in organizations are crucial for ensuring the integration and synergy of the elements specified in the marketing mix model. These aspects must work together harmoniously and complement each other effectively in all marketing strategies and plans (Abratt & Bendixen, 2018; Deepak & Jeyakumar, 2019).

IoT has emerged as a prominent phenomenon in the field of digital technology over the last five years (Colwyn, 2015). Nevertheless, the discourse surrounding the utilization of the Internet of Things (IoT) in the field of marketing has been notably constrained. Hence, this chapter delves into the utilization of the Internet of Things (IoTs) in the field of marketing, with a particular focus on its impact on the marketing mix, commonly known as the 4Ps. Consequently, our study provides four distinct contributions to the existing body of literature. This study contributes to the advancement of knowledge regarding the potential of IoT technology in facilitating the digitalization of corporate operations for management and marketing objectives. Managers and marketers can utilize existing data to suggest specific technological tactics that align with common managerial tasks, aiming to rejuvenate a corporation. This chapter's goal is to review the body of research on the connection between the Internet of Things and the marketing mix.

LITERATURE

IoT

According to Madakam *et al.* (2015), IoT has significantly transformed the information and communication technology (ICT) landscape by merging the realms of communication, particularly the Internet, and physical items, sometimes referred to as "things" (Madakam *et al.*, 2015). The Internet of Things (IoT) undoubtedly represents a highly useful instrument for comprehending client data and enhancing the efficacy of marketing initiatives. Monitoring consumer activity on their smart devices provides valuable insights into the items and services that may pique their interest for potential purchase. Intelligent gadgets possess the capability to store and manage a substantial volume of information, which can be leveraged to examine significant insights pertaining to clients' shopping and evaluating behaviors. Furthermore, such data has the potential to provide valuable information on customers' daily lifestyles (Simões *et al.*, 2019). The primary objective of the IoTs is to establish connectivity on a global scale by collecting data from tangible objects (Erboz, 2017). According to Rahman and Rahmani (2017), computers and other advanced gadgets acquire data and utilize it in order to make informed choices about operations. The implementation of the Internet of Things (IoT) technology enhances the agility and integration of company activities, leading to the attainment of a competitive advantage through the utilization of intelligent computing. According to Akhtar *et al.* (2018), the future significance of enterprises' IoT capabilities lies mostly in their capacity for flexibility and informed decision-making.

Marketing Mix (7Ps)

The marketing mix is a fundamental concept in the field of marketing. It refers to a set of controllable marketing tools that a company uses to serve its markets. Marketing includes the activities involved in advertising, selling, and distributing goods or services to consumers. Marketing comprises a comprehensive range of activities and is frequently executed by both internal and external stakeholders, including advertising, social media experts, sales representatives, and marketing professionals. Marketing is an essential corporate endeavor that plays a pivotal role in facilitating the creation of customer value and fostering robust customer relationships. The primary objective of this study is to explore and devise effective techniques that will assist organizations in enhancing their sales income for their products and services, thus enabling them to attain a more prominent market share.

The marketing mix's beginnings may be traced back to the year 1960 when it was initially published in E. Jerome McCarthy's well-acclaimed publication, Basic Marketing - A Managerial Approach. Subsequently, the phrase "marketing mix" was formally established by Neil Borden, a renowned Harvard professor, in his seminal work titled "The Concept of the Marketing Mix", published in 1964. Borden explicated that his concept was derived from the influence of his colleague, James Culliton (1959), who drew a parallel between accomplished marketers and skilled culinary experts. According to Sahaf (2019), Culliton drew a parallel between great chefs and successful marketers, highlighting their shared approach of adhering to a recipe while also being open to experimentation with new ingredients and making real-time adjustments in response to market dynamics and client preferences. Borden identifies several factors that have the potential to influence the marketing mix, such as customer shopping incentives, the competitive environment, and governmental laws. The enduring nature of the four P's in the marketing field is evident as they continue to retain significance despite the rapid advancement of digitalization. This can be attributed to their robust basic principles, as highlighted by Yasar (2023).

The marketing mix, also referred to as the four P's of marketing, encompasses the fundamental components of a marketing plan, namely product, price, location, and promotion. By diligently considering the four fundamental elements of the marketing mix, a corporation can optimize its prospects of garnering client recognition and achieving product purchases. According to Sahaf (2019), products can be defined as commodities and services that effectively address problems and fulfill the demands of consumers. A product has the potential to possess tangibility, exemplified by entities like vehicles or articles of apparel, or intangibility, as demonstrated by services like cruises or house cleaning. A product's success can be attributed to its ability to either address an unmet need in the market or provide a distinctive experience that generates high demand. Price refers to the monetary value that consumers are required to pay in exchange for a product. In the context of product marketing, it is crucial to establish a pricing strategy that aligns with prevailing market dynamics and remains accessible to consumers while simultaneously ensuring profitability for the enterprise (Yasar, 2023). The price of a product is subject to variation depending on the interplay between supply and demand, as well as the specific sales cycle of the product. Certain firms may choose to decrease their prices in order to remain competitive within the market, whilst others may want to increase their prices, particularly if they are focused on promoting a premium brand. The location and method by which customers acquire the goods or services is referred to as the point of purchase. Additionally, it encompasses the aspects of product storage and manufacturing location. The advent of digital transformation has revolutionized the methods by which items are marketed and sold, including many channels such as internet platforms, local retail establishments, and international manufacturers. This marketing plan also takes into account the advertising channels and formats used to promote the product, including periodicals, online advertisements, radio, infomercials, and film product placements. Promotion entails effectively communicating the intended message to the designated audience at the appropriate moment. According to Yasar (2023), utilizing this method effectively disseminates information and serves as an efficient means to execute sales promotions and establish consumer connections. The primary objective of a promotional strategy is to effectively communicate to consumers the value proposition of a certain product and the rationale behind choosing it over alternative offerings. Marketing communications is a fundamental aspect of the field of marketing, whereby product promotions are strategically disseminated across many media to convey targeted and significant advertising messages. According to Yasar (2023), several marketing strategies can be employed, such as word-of-mouth seeding, social networking, Instagram campaigns, print marketing, television advertising, email marketing campaigns, and social media marketing.

The publication titled "Marketing Strategies and Organizational Structures for Service Firms" by Bernard Booms and Mary Jo Bitner in 1981 introduced the concept of the 7Ps of the marketing mix. The revised iteration of the original 4Ps framework has three more elements, namely people, process, and physical evidence. Individuals play a crucial role in the delivery of any product or service. They encompass all individuals engaged in the buyer's journey, including the buyer themselves, as well as staff, partners, consumers, and the interconnections formed among them. The quality of service perceived by the consumer can be influenced by the mood, character, and conduct exhibited during the service delivery process. According to Carniel (2022), when a product or service aims to cater to a larger number of consumers concurrently, it has the potential to shape their collective experience. Processes encompass a range of mechanisms, planning activities, and decision-making processes that are implemented to facilitate the efficient and effective provision of a product or service (Carniel, 2022). Physical evidence encompasses the various environmental components that include consumers during the delivery of a service or product. Carniel (2022) examines the factors that contribute to both positive and bad outcomes in the delivery experience. For instance, elements such as interior design, color schemes, spatial arrangement, equipment selection, furniture choices, and facility amenities.

IOTS AND MARKETING MIX

Products

The offerings can encompass either services or tangible goods. Business-support services encompass a range of activities aimed at facilitating the growth and implementation of digital products and services within enterprises. Business-support services encompass a range of offerings, including the provision of internet design, online hosting and maintenance services, and the creation of digital content, such as audio and video recordings and multimedia development. Customer service activities encompass a range of actions aimed at facilitating consumer access to and utilization of online resources and digital information.

Consumer services commonly encompass various entities, including internet service providers (ISPs), information portals, and media suppliers, such as electronic radio and TV broadcasters. Digital communication offerings encompass the administration of technological infrastructure and operational protocols that provide virtual communications for both corporate and consumer purposes. According to Kleindle & Burrow (2005), the term "product" pertains to the tangible or intangible offering that is being promoted to consumers by IoT applications investments and challenges for enterprises. This offering is intended to be consumed by the target audience of The Internet of Things IoT Applications investments and challenges for enterprises (Groucutt & Hopkins, 2015). The primary objective of IoT applications expenditures and difficulties for organizations is to address market needs and demands while also striving to generate demand through the provision of a distinctive and satisfactory customer experience (Sahaf, 2019). The implementation of production-line monitoring for the purpose of proactive equipment repair upon detection of an imminent defect has the potential to confer a competitive edge to manufacturers. Sensors have the capability to identify instances where a plant's production is potentially compromised. By leveraging sensor warnings, manufacturers may expedite the process of inspecting equipment precision and, if required, temporarily remove it from production for necessary repairs. The implementation of this method has been shown to yield enhanced asset performance management and cost reductions (Terra, 2022). When things possess the ability to see their surroundings and engage in communication, they assume the role of instruments for comprehending intricacy and promptly reacting to it, frequently in a live setting. The physical world is increasingly assuming the characteristics of an information system. Sensors and actuators that are integrated within tangible entities, interconnected *via* both wired and wireless networks, generate substantial volumes of data that are subsequently transmitted to computer systems for analysis. The utilization of ingestible pill-shaped microcameras has been developed to facilitate non-invasive identification of the origin of diseases or malfunctioning organs within the human body. These microcameras are designed to traverse the digestive tract, capturing images at various stages of the journey, so enabling medical professionals to make accurate diagnoses without resorting to surgical procedures. According to Darius (2023), the ongoing process of downsizing enables the potential insertion of "bots" into the bloodstream for the purpose of capturing images or monitoring blood vessels in order to identify the origins of issues. In order to navigate effectively, individuals must possess the knowledge and skills to execute a reversal or backward movement or alternatively, undergo a process of dissolution or surgical extraction. Given the established position of IoT commerce within its market, there is potential for expansion into adjacent areas. This expansion would cater to customers who already utilize complementary items from other companies in order to maximize the value derived from their purchases.

The principal factor influencing consumer purchasing behavior is closely associated with the quality and characteristics of a business's products. According to a study conducted by Kleindle & Burrow (2005), the attributes of a product significantly influence its effectiveness in online marketing endeavors. According to the study conducted by Kiang *et al.* (2000), the Internet is utilized to alter the configuration of certain goods. Examples of transformations in the physical manifestation of conventional goods include electronic books, electronic tickets, digital photos, and online bill payment systems. Certain consumers perceive the novel iterations as more gratifying, but others exhibit a preference for the products in their unaltered states. According to the study conducted by Kleindle & Burrow in 2005, IoT serves as a platform for the marketing of a diverse array of items, encompassing both consumable and durable goods. The breadth of services marketed on the Internet encompasses a variety of offerings, including online newspapers as well as comprehensive business consultation services, according to the study conducted by Kiang *et al.* (2000).

Pricing

Dynamic pricing can be employed when purchasing habits are identified, whether through online platforms or in physical retail establishments. Dynamic pricing differs from fixed or administered pricing, where a predetermined price is affixed to a product, and all buyers are charged the same amount. Dynamic pricing is a pricing strategy wherein the determination of price adjustments, whether they be increased or decreased, is contingent upon the level of demand at the time of purchase. Dynamic pricing has been effectively implemented in the realm of baseball. In contrast to the prevailing practice of scalpers profiting from high-demand sporting events, an analytical model is employed to assess the influence of various factors on game attendance. These factors include weather conditions, the day of the week, and the time of day, which collectively impact the rate at which tickets are being sold, the availability of ticket inventory, and the level of publicity generated by a player nearing a significant milestone. Consequently, these factors influence the demand for tickets and the extent to which fans are willing to pay elevated prices (Darius, 2023). In contrast, in situations when ticket sales exhibit sluggishness and a surplus of unoccupied seats is evident, it can be inferred that the weather conditions are likely to be characterized by chilly temperatures and precipitation, resulting in a decline in ticket prices. Nonetheless, should the cost of a single game go below the mean price of a season ticket, the team will encounter challenges in selling future season tickets. In a study by Harris & Dennis (2002), the predominant emphasis in the realm of e-pricing theory has been on the examination of price competition and price sensitivity in the online context compared to the offline environment. The notion that online search costs are reduced has generated significant scholarly attention as researchers seek strategies to mitigate online price sensitivity and foster product differentiation. According to the findings of Mahajan and Venkatesh (2000), Peterson *et al.* have argued that Internet-based marketing can lead to intense price competition in cases when products or services lack substantial differences. According to the study conducted by Kiang *et al.* (2000), the implementation of dynamic pricing necessitates a substantial amount of data. The implementation of numerous sensors in manufacturing processes enables enhanced precision in control, leading to heightened efficiency and cost reduction. Given the decrease in costs, marketers are presented with a wider array of options. These options include reducing the price of the product, improving the quality of the product, allocating additional funds towards advertising and promotional activities, or enhancing the speed and quality of product delivery. The progression of wireless networking technologies and the increased uniformity of communications protocols have facilitated the acquisition of data from sensors in virtually any location and at any given moment. The use and utilization of progressively smaller silicon chips for sensors are on the rise, resulting in enhanced functionalities and wider acceptance. This trend has led to a decrease in production costs, thereby influencing the pricing dynamics. Certain insurance companies have proposed the installation of location sensors in the vehicles of their customers. The utilization of sensors allows the insurance business to establish the insurance premium for a driver by analyzing the manner in which a vehicle is operated, including factors such as the geographical locations visited, the velocity of travel, road conditions, and levels of traffic congestion. Pricing can be determined by the specific risk associated with operating the vehicle rather than relying on factors such as the driver's age, gender, or commuting distance.

The price is an additional factor that significantly influences the online purchasing decisions of the majority of consumers. Fagerstron & Ghinea (2011) conducted a study. The concept of marketing pricing remains unchanged, as it is determined by the price that customers are willing to pay. This willingness is influenced by various factors, including the company's reputation, brand image, and the perceived value of the product. E-commerce has a significant impact by expediting and enhancing the accessibility of pricing and competitor information, resulting in accelerated market dynamics and potentially improved efficiency. Consequently, there exists a propensity for prices to gradually align towards reduced values.

Distribution

The concept of distribution refers to the manner in which something is spread out or allocated among individuals. The data can determine the appropriate storage methods for products prior to transportation, including considerations of geographic locations and shelf placement. The implementation of RFID (radio-frequency identification) sensors on products has the potential to significantly improve inventory management, resulting in cost reduction. Robotic systems engaged in product transportation exhibit a notable absence of back injuries since they are not susceptible to such physical ailments. Additionally, the stock rotation process is executed in a manner that aligns with established standards, ensuring optimal product freshness and quality. Furthermore, the analysis and anticipation of demand patterns enable expedited delivery, hence enhancing overall operational efficiency. The utilization of IoT applications in transportation and logistics systems enables the effective rerouting of inventory-carrying fleets across different modes of transportation. This is achieved by the deployment of data sensors that consider factors such as weather conditions, vehicle characteristics, and driver attributes. The integration of sensors inside the inventory itself enables the monitoring and tracing of goods, as well as the management of temperature conditions. Temperature-sensitive inventory is prevalent in various industries, including pharmaceuticals, food and beverage, and flowers. In this context, the utilization of IoT monitoring applications that provide timely alerts in the event of temperature fluctuations, which can potentially jeopardize the integrity of the products, would be highly advantageous (Oracle, 2022). The distribution process plays a crucial role in every marketing transaction. Typically, it entails the participation of multiple enterprises. The completion of the task at hand may need a significant amount of time, potentially spanning several days or even weeks, during which a multitude of actions will need to be undertaken. The cost of distribution is high. It has the potential to constitute more than 50 percent of the ultimate cost of a product. The implementation of an e-commerce strategy does not result in the elimination of distribution activities within a business. According to the study conducted by Kleindle & Burrow (2005), the distribution aspect holds significant importance within the realm of e-business due to three key rationales. Initially, modest-sized local enterprises have the potential to expand their market reach and engage in exporting activities. Furthermore, numerous e-businesses strive to attain a competitive edge by leveraging e-systems to streamline the distribution chain. As an illustration, Dell engages in direct supply to clients, bypassing the involvement of distributors, wholesalers, or retailers. Thirdly, the aspect of distribution has been subject to severe criticism in relation to certain e-businesses due to their failure to provide satisfactory customer service (Harris & Dennis, 2002).

Promotion

Promotional billboards often consist of static printed pictures that remain stationary for a duration of at least 30 days, often succumbing to the effects of weathering over time. The utilization of intelligent billboards has the potential to exhibit advertisements for a length that aligns with the level of traffic congestion. The collection of eye-tracking data can be facilitated by the act of a driver or passenger directing their gaze toward the advertisement. According to Tudor *et al.* (2021), cameras possess the capability to capture images of automobiles. By employing image recognition techniques, it becomes possible to discern the specific makes and models of these cars. This information may be used to enhance the precision of demographic targeting strategies associated with particular vehicles. Promotions across various mediums, ranging from online platforms to physical outdoor billboards, are influenced by the IoT.Yahoo has obtained patents for 40 distinct characteristics of Smart Billboards. These billboards incorporate sensors that track the time of day and day of the week as a vehicle goes by. Additionally, they have the capability to collaborate with advertising exchanges in order to share information and deliver targeted advertisements to individuals' devices, such as tablets, phones, smartwatches, and TVs. In the context of conventional marketing, advertising is characterized by its impersonal nature, as it entails one-way mass communication that is financially supported by sponsors. Telemarketing and direct mail are implemented as strategies to enhance the efficacy of advertising by including personalized approaches. The efficacy of these direct marketing strategies is somewhat satisfactory, yet, they are characterized by high costs, sluggishness, and a lack of genuine one-to-one interactivity. The advent of the Internet has introduced the notion of interactive marketing, hence facilitating direct interaction between advertisers and customers. According to Turban and King (2003), this technology enables the retrieval of information without being limited by geographical boundaries and has the potential for delivering messages that are enriched with color, sound, animation effects, and interactive capabilities. The internet's interactive nature has enabled a higher level of customer assistance and market activity compared to traditional media (Kurtz & Boone, 2006).

People

End nodes are entities that are interconnected over the internet for the purpose of exchanging information and engaging in various activities. Illustrative instances encompass social networks, as well as health and fitness sensors, among other exemplifications. The process of servicing entails a direct engagement between service providers and consumers through the use of Internet of Things (IoT) applications, hence expanding the potential for subjective experiences. The crucial characteristics encompassed in this context are appearances, interaction, discretion, consumer engagement, behavior, and attitude toward service.

Physicals

The brand image of a product can be significantly influenced by the setting, design, and style of the workplace. Physical sensors, gadgets, actuators, and other components are responsible for the generation of data or reception of information from external sources. Illustrative instances encompass intelligent thermostats and technological devices.

Processes

Standardized protocols are commonly implemented in instances that include policy, procedures, systems, and consumer engagement to ensure consistency during service delivery. Utilizing the interconnectedness of IoT data, objects, and individuals to enhance value. Illustrative instances encompass the utilization of intelligent fitness equipment and online social platforms to promote pertinent services, such as healthcare services, to potential clientele. Mostly, raw data from marketing intelligence is subjected to analysis and IoT-based processing in order to derive valuable information that can facilitate informed decision-making and the implementation of effective control measures.

Implications

In relation to IoT, the primary impediment for managers appears to be the cognitive processes of individuals responsible for programming machines/IoT to generate desired outcomes, specifically in relation to the analysis of vast quantities of data collected on a continuous basis. The ultimate objective of this chapter for managers is to obtain the necessary outcomes for making optimal business and marketing decisions. The wide range of applications available presents further opportunities for academia and companies to explore and address their own requirements, as well as the needs of consumers. In the contemporary marketing landscape, it is imperative for marketers to critically examine the ways in which businesses may enhance customer satisfaction through the utilization of IoT technology. The integration of sensors within the frames of reading glasses would provide significant support to individuals who are new to wearing glasses and frequently misplace them.

CONCLUSION

The significant influence of the IoTs on marketing and business has been brought about by its quick advancements. The chapter examined the interconnections between IoT and several marketing elements, including product, price, promotion, place, process, physical evidence, and people. The untapped potential benefits of IoT in the field of marketing have yet to be fully realized. In order to effectively leverage the transformative benefits of IoT in the development of novel products and services, it is imperative to conduct extensive research with a focus on practical applications. It may be reasonably inferred that there is a high level of certainty regarding the potential for advancements in the IoT, considering the significant influence it has already exerted on the domain of marketing. This chapter provides a comprehensive analysis of the existing body of research pertaining to IoT and its impact on the marketing mix. IoT should be recognized as a comprehensive area of study due to its extensive impact on several facets of human existence, encompassing the marketing of products and services. There exist specific categories of consumers who engage in online purchasing. A demographic of individuals possess a high level of comfort and familiarity with technology and innovation. If the business anticipates that consumers will utilize the Internet as a means of purchasing its products, it is advisable to focus marketing endeavors on innovators and early adopters. The advent of the internet and IoT has introduced novel concerns that necessitate careful consideration and might necessitate a reassessment of the current marketing mix. The implementation of IoT technology enables enterprises to engage in the mass customization of a diverse array of products. The utilization of the Internet facilitates the expeditious dissemination of pricing and competition information, hence enhancing the transparency of markets. Consequently, market forces are inclined to operate with greater celerity and potentially heightened efficiency. The advent of the Internet has introduced the notion of interactive marketing, hence facilitating direct interaction between advertisers and customers. IoT enables the retrieval of information without being limited by geographical boundaries. Additionally, it provides the potential for transmitting messages that are enriched with visual, auditory, and animated elements, along with the capability for interactive exchanges. Through the utilization of the Internet, manufacturers have the ability to engage in direct sales to consumers and offer online customer support services. In this context, the conventional intermediaries are eradicated or subjected to disintermediation. It is imperative for managers to possess a comprehensive understanding of the concept of value, including its definition, the processes through which it is generated, and the methods by which it can be augmented. IoT has numerous prospects for enterprises to enhance economic utility and, consequently, enhance consumer happiness.

The wide array of tools and platforms currently available to businesses has significantly enhanced our comprehension of clients, facilitating the connection between customers and prospects with products and services that enhance their quality of life. Nevertheless, the efficacy of the campaigns we implement remains deeply rooted in the fundamental principles of marketing, namely product, price, place, and promotion. Proficient marketers have the ability to effectively integrate these concepts with the aforementioned strategies in order to get the anticipated, financially advantageous results that their enterprises want.

REFERENCES

Carniel, A. (2022). The ultimate guide to marketing mix: 4Ps, 7Ps, 8Ps, 4Cs, 7Cs. Available from: https://www.albertocarniel.com/post/marketing-mix.

Colwyn, S. (2015). What will the Internet of Things mean for marketers? [Infographic]. Available from: https://www.smartinsights.com/digital-marketing-platforms/marketo-internet-things-infographic/.

Culliton, J.W. (1959). A marketing analysis of religion. *Bus. Horiz., 2*(1), 85-92. [http://dx.doi.org/10.1016/0007-6813(59)90046-1]

Darius, J. (2023). 6 Ways Digital Marketing Benefits from the Internet of Things.

Fagerstrøm, A., Ghinea, G. (2011). On the motivating impact of price and online recommendations at the point of online purchase. *Int. J. Inf. Manage., 31*(2), 103-110. [http://dx.doi.org/10.1016/j.ijinfomgt.2010.10.013]

Groucutt, J., Hopkins, C. (2015). *Marketing.* London: Macmillan International Higher Education.

Harris, L., Dennis, C. (2002). *Marketing the e-Business..* London, England: Routledge.

Kiang, M.Y., Raghu, T.S., Shang, K.H.M. (2000). Marketing on the Internet — who can benefit from an online marketing approach? *Decis. Support Syst., 27*(4), 383-393. [http://dx.doi.org/10.1016/S0167-9236(99)00062-7]

Kleindle, B., Burrow, J. (2005). *E-Commerce Marketing. South-Western..* United States: Thomson.

Oracle (2022). What is IoT? Available from: https://www.oracle.com/ro/internet-of-things/what-is-iot/.

Sahaf, A. (2019). Strategic marketing: Making decisions for strategic advantage. New Delhi, India: PHI Learning Pvt. Ltd. Available from: https://attentioninsight.com/6-ways-digital-marketing-benefits-frm-the-internet-of-things/.

Tudor, A.I.M., Chiṭu, I.B., Dovleac, L., Brătucu, G. (2021). IoT Technologies as Instruments for SMEs' Innovation and Sustainable Growth. *Sustainability, 13*(11), 6357. [http://dx.doi.org/10.3390/su13116357]

Terra, J. (2022). SimpliLearn, 8 Real-World IoT Applications in 2020, Last updated on Mar 18, 2022. Available from: https://www.simplilearn.com/iot-applications-article.

Yasar, K. (2023). 4 P's marketing mix. Available from: https://www.techtarget.com/ whatis/definition/Four-Ps.

CHAPTER 6

Place/Distribution and the Internet of Things

Mohammed Majeed[1,*], **Ahmed Sakara**[1], **Alhassan Yahaya**[1] and **Mohammed Abdul-Basit Fuseini**[1]

[1] *Department of Marketing, Tamale Technical University, Tamale, Ghana*

Abstract: The Internet of Things (IoT) is a remarkable technological advancement that facilitates the seamless integration of computing devices for the purpose of transmitting data across a network, eliminating the need for direct human-to-human or human-t--computer engagements. This chapter intends to look at how IoT impacts the distribution of firms' products. The implementation of IoT-based advanced distribution, materials handling equipment, and sensors in warehouses has the potential to significantly transform operations, resulting in increased efficiency, cost-effectiveness, and productivity. The integration of the Internet of Things (IoT) into warehouse operations encompasses the real-time monitoring of equipment, goods, pallets, and personnel, as well as the measurement of their performance.

Keywords: Distribution, Internet, Internet of things, Place, SCM, Technology.

INTRODUCTION

The pervasive integration of new technologies into various aspects of daily life has contributed to the prevailing notion that for every societal concern, there exists an information and communication technology (ICT) solution capable of effectively addressing it. The "Internet of Things" (IoT) has emerged as a frequently advocated answer in contemporary discourse. The perceived universal remedy within the realm of information and communication technology (ICT) encompasses various facets and is associated with diverse technological alternatives, frequently exhibiting significant disparities. The Internet of Things (IoT) is a remarkable technological advancement that facilitates the seamless integration of computing devices for the purpose of transmitting data across a network, eliminating the need for direct human-to-human or human-to-computer engagements (Atzori *et al.*, 2017). This technology has the potential to create numerous opportunities within the context of contemporary smart grid systems and energy markets. The impact of the Internet of Things (IoT) on several aspects

* **Corresponding author Mohammed Majeed:** Department of Marketing, Tamale Technical University, Tamale, Ghana; E-mail: tunteya14june@gmail.com

Mohammed Majeed, Jonas Yomboi, Sulemana Ibrahim & Esther Asiedu (Eds.)

of the smart grid, including smart cities, smart homes, home energy management systems, energy harvesting systems, intelligent networks of sensors, and centralized generation (CG), has been discussed in the literature (Kabalci *et al.*, 2019). The Internet of Things (IoT) offers significant benefits by fostering increased innovation and competitiveness within the realm of electronic marketing and distribution. IoT technologies employed in the realm of digital marketing lack a comprehensive and integrated perspective when it comes to identifying the advancements in electronic marketing. Numerous marketing platforms have acknowledged the disadvantages associated with forming distribution agreements with marketing firms (Joghee, 2021). According to a recent report by Gartner (2020), the Internet of Things (IoT) is projected to have a significant impact on enterprises, with its adoption rate expected to reach 26 billion devices by 2020. According to Gartner, it has been projected that providers of Internet of Things (IoT) products and services will create additional revenue surpassing $300 billion by the year 2020. This revenue is expected to be mostly derived from the provision of services. The projected outcome of this development is a global economic value-add of $1.9 trillion, achieved through the sale of products and services across various end markets. It is imperative for businesses to seize this chance for substantial expansion in order to remain competitive. The integration of technological capabilities within gadgets has the potential to significantly influence supply networks. The comprehensive integration of sensors into every stage of the supply chain, encompassing raw materials, product components, finished items, individual cartons, containers, shipments, and delivered orders, will result in a profound transformation of the whole supply chain and distribution process. The concept of the Internet of Things (IoT) involves the integration of intelligent devices and sensors with advanced data analytics and cloud computing technologies. According to Schwaderer (2015), the emergence of this paradigm shift introduces novel complexities pertaining to software delivery, upgrades, and security. The utilization of IoT technology is necessary for several applications, such as enhancing energy efficiency, augmenting the proportion of renewable energy, and mitigating the environmental consequences associated with energy consumption. Therefore, the Internet of Things (IoT) has the potential to facilitate the transformation of energy networks, particularly distribution networks, from a centralized structure to a distributed, intelligent, and integrated distribution system, which is essential for the successful implementation of renewable energy sources (RESs) like wind and solar energy (Yu *et al.*, 2015). Furthermore, it facilitates the transition of multiple small-scale energy consumers into prosumers by consolidating their energy generation and optimizing their energy consumption in a manner that benefits the overall grid system. The realization of automation, integration, and control processes within the grid network can be facilitated by employing Internet of

Things (IoT)-based systems, which rely on the utilization of sensors and diverse communication technologies. The Internet of Things (IoT) revolution is expected to have a significant impact on enterprise applications and supply chain solutions. This revolution will involve the intelligent connection of people, processes, data, and physical objects through the use of devices and sensors. The implementation of automation in the manufacturing process and the enhancement of visibility within warehouses are increasingly seen as essential requirements. The utilization of strategically deployed devices and systems in the production chain enables the creation, processing, and analysis of data, resulting in a notable reduction in visibility gaps and the introduction of substantial flexibility. Evolving solutions facilitate the utilization of simulation, predictive capabilities, and modeling techniques to effectively mitigate costs and enhance service and quality levels in real time. The term "place" within the marketing mix pertains to the distribution channels and methods utilized to deliver products to the end consumer. Organizations strategically develop communication channels in order to effectively reach a large client base while minimizing costs. The advent of the internet has significantly altered the positioning component inside the marketing mix. The concept of the point of purchase can be categorized into various types, including seller-controlled sites, third-party hosted seller-oriented sites, third-party hosted consumer-seller neutral sites, purchaser-controlled sites, and buyer-controlled sites. Organizations are currently engaged in the development of websites that are tailored to meet the distinct needs and preferences of individual countries. The aforementioned criteria may pertain to language, product assortment, and cultural distinctions. The internet has also brought about changes in the distribution methods. Organizations must make a strategic determination regarding the distribution of goods, weighing the option of utilizing intermediaries vs adopting a direct-to-consumer delivery approach. Organizations can employ a hybrid approach that combines both intermediary and direct distribution methods. This chapter intends to look at how IoT impacts the distribution of firms' products.

LITERATURE

IoT

The Internet of Things (IoT) leverages Internet infrastructure to establish connectivity among tangible entities, sometimes referred to as "things". This technology is currently in its early stages of development. It encompasses a range of physical devices that can be employed in various applications, including both domestic appliances and industrial machinery. These devices have the capability to deliver significant data and a range of services to individuals through the use of appropriate sensors and internet connections. For instance, the implementation of an intelligent energy usage control system in buildings can effectively mitigate energy expenses. The Internet of Things (IoT) encompasses a wide range of software programs, including but not limited to transportation, production, and the building sector. These applications have the potential to enhance the administration of energy and environmental monitoring, as well as facilitate the provision of drone-based services (Motlagh *et al.*, 2020).

Place/Distribution

A place/distribution/location refers to a commercial setting where individuals have the opportunity to purchase a certain product or service. The means of providing access to a product or service might take on physical forms, such as a brick-and-mortar store, or intangible forms, such as an e-commerce platform. The crucial aspect is the provision of accessibility (Carniel, 2022). The concept of place encompasses the strategic decision-making process of selecting the appropriate location for the distribution and sale of items. The principal objective of trade channel management is to guarantee the timely and convenient availability of the product to the client. Additionally, it encompasses the process of making decisions pertaining to the strategic placement and pricing strategies of both wholesale and retail establishments. The determination of distribution methods, such as outsourcing or business transport fleets, is made following a comprehensive evaluation of costs and benefits. The study conducted by Motlagh *et al.* (2020) incorporates specific information regarding the allocation of shelf space for the product in department stores.

Place/Distribution Internet of Things (DIoT)

The concept of place in the 4Ps model of the marketing mix primarily pertains to the specific locations where a firm inventories its product and service offerings, with the aim of ensuring accessibility and facilitating consumer purchasing. The sales strategy for growth in an electronic company is determined by the particular characteristics of the good or service group being implemented. In the context of information products, the duration and expenses associated with order fulfillment are relatively short. Conversely, for physical goods, the costs are contingent upon factors such as the product's shelf life, the selected transportation strategy, the quantity of the order, and the desired speed of shipment. It is essential to provide clients with prior notification regarding the requirements for delivery and associated costs (Pogorelova *et al.*, 2016). In the realm of online shopping, the place of sale refers to a digital platform, such as a website or a social network marketplace, where transactions occur. The latter, which serves as the main point for interacting with the intended consumers, also fulfills promotional purposes. In contemporary business practices, the point of a transaction can manifest as a communal platform accommodating a multitude of sellers, either operating under a standardized pricing structure (aliexpress.com) or engaging in auction-based transactions (ebay.com). The place, in this particular instance, is characterized by the extensive availability of sales channels for both buyers and sellers, which is a significant attribute. The domain of in-transit visibility is expected to be significantly impacted by the Internet of Things (IoT) (Shankar, 2016). The utilization of cloud-based GPS and Radio Frequency Identification (RFID) technologies plays a crucial role in enhancing in-transit visibility. According to Atzori, Iera, and Morabito (2010), the utilization of RFID technology enables the instantaneous processing of information pertaining to all activities within the supply chain. This advancement enables firms to strategically optimize their distribution routes, ensuring that inventory is consistently positioned in the appropriate location, at the precise moment, and in the optimal quantity. The development of automated ordering and system technologies has the potential to enable the implementation of automated transportation procedures, which in turn can accurately forecast the expected time of arrival. This enables organizations to effectively target customers with more precision, as the reduction in response time to customer needs is substantial. Furthermore, the implementation of tracking and tracing systems can significantly improve customer service by providing customers with real-time information regarding the precise location and status of their items during the whole delivery process. Moreover, this will enable organizations to generate increased revenue as a result of the very brief duration between identifying a particular client requirement and providing a response to it. Additionally, the optimization and automation of inventory and transportation processes can lead to cost reduction and enable organizations to enhance their profitability. The incorporation of Internet of Things (IoT) technology into supply chain management offers the benefits of process automation and the ability to monitor critical factors such as temperature control, traffic conditions, and driver-specific data. These factors have the potential to significantly impact product quality. The investments and problems associated with Internet of Things (IoT) applications in organizations necessitate the inclusion of all feasible locations that are readily accessible and available to the target audience of the company (Iacobucci, 2021; Išoraitė, 2016). The proliferation of technology has led to the expansion of Internet of Things (IoT) applications, expenditures, and problems for organizations. This expansion has not only encompassed traditional brick-an--mortar retail spaces but also modern Omni channel retail platforms (Iacobucci, 2021).

HOW IS IOT USED IN DISTRIBUTION/PLACE

Retailing and E-Commerce

Conventional brick and mortar venues, commonly known as physical retail outlets, remain the preferred sites for product placement according to research on investments and problems in Internet of Things (IoT) technologies for organizations (Iacobucci, 2021; Groucutt & Hopkins, 2015; Abratt & Bendixen, 2018). These encompass retail stores, high-end markets, and smaller grocery stores, all of which provide enhanced access as well as availability of resources and problems related to Internet of Things (IoT) applications for organizations' goods and services to their intended audience. Physical retail stores see a greater number of visitors and facilitate direct engagement between the business and its product offers with consumers (Groucutt & Hopkins, 2015). Enterprises invest in and face issues related to the applications of the Internet of Things (IoT). Additionally, they distribute their products through e-commerce retail platforms, including Amazon. This phenomenon enables organizations to make higher expenditures on the Internet of Things (IoT) applications and overcome the hurdles associated with them. Consequently, it facilitates greater entry and penetration into additional markets, including secondary consumer groups. In addition, e-commerce retailing has been found to offer greater cost-effectiveness in terms of investments and issues related to the Internet of Things (IoT) applications, as supported by scholarly sources (Wu & Li,2018; Cherney,2018; Rosengren,2017).

Factory of the Future or Smart Manufacturing

The concept of factory of the future or smart manufacturing is gaining traction in several manufacturing industries. This entails the use of sophisticated technologies, utilization of the Internet of Things, and the application of analytics data to enhance productivity and responsiveness in manufacturing processes (Chatterjee, 2016). In the realm of industrial automation, the integration of Internet of Things (IoT) technology into factory equipment and manufacturing units enables the seamless transmission of crucial data such as temperature readings and machine utilization metrics. Additionally, this integration empowers the ability to modify equipment settings and enhance process workflows for optimal efficiency. According to Chatterjee (2016), Internet of Things (IoT) devices possess the capability to provide notifications regarding the expiration dates of lifetimes and maintenance requirements. This functionality aims to enhance the overall performance and efficiency of supply chains. The Internet of Things (IoT) is playing a significant role in supporting the food processing and manufacturing industry through the continuous monitoring of factory climate conditions and the detection of allergies.

Prioritizing Health

The importance of prioritizing health cannot be overstated. The prioritization of employee wellness takes precedence for distribution managers, notwithstanding the significance of optimizing operations and minimizing theft within a warehouse. It is imperative for employees to experience a sense of security inside their workplace environment, wherein adherence to social distancing protocols is evident. This assurance is crucial in enabling employees to depart from work with a tranquil state of mind, knowing that they can safely reunite with their families. The implementation of Internet of Things (IoT) technology has the potential to assist managers in safeguarding the well-being and security of their employees. This can be achieved by strategically deploying IoT-enabled occupancy management sensors across various facilities (Groucutt & Hopkins, 2015; Chernev, 2018). Consequently, supervisors will possess real-time visibility about the individuals who have completed check-ins at several warehouses. This information will provide management with valuable insights into the real-time occupancy of a warehouse and the determination of whether the facility has hit its maximum capacity. In the context of warehouse management, the utilization of Internet of Things (IoT)-enabled sensors for occupancy management can offer an additional capability of promptly conducting contact tracing within the premises in the event of an employee testing positive for the virus. Sensors that are powered by the Internet of Things (IoT) and are affixed to workstations have the capability to check if employees are adhering to social distancing protocols. In the event that stations necessitate sanitization, these sensors can promptly alert management.

Firm's Website

Furthermore, alongside collaborating with other electronic retailers, the Internet of Things (IoT) applications, investments, and challenges for enterprises also oversee the processing of orders *via* its own website. This platform enables consumers to directly place orders for the products offered by the Internet of Things (IoT) applications, investments, and challenges for enterprises. The use of Internet of Things (IoT) applications provides organizations with enhanced control over stock and inventory management, as well as distribution networks. This, in turn, facilitates the development of more robust relationships with consumers. In addition, firms face both investments and obstacles in relation to the applications of the Internet of Things (IoT), which includes the limited acceptance of orders through social media pages and platforms (Wu & Li, 2018; Baines, Fill, & Rosengren, 2017).

Temperature and Humidity Sensors

The utilization of Internet of Things (IoT) connected sensors presents an opportunity for successfully tracking the environmental parameters of commodities during their transit inside the supply chain. The significance of this matter is particularly pronounced in the case of commodities that are susceptible to alterations in temperature or humidity, such as perishable food products or medications. The utilization of Internet of Things (IoT)-enabled sensors has the potential to facilitate the monitoring of items' condition during their transit inside the supply chain. For instance, sensors possess the capability to identify whether a package has incurred any form of damage or if there has been an occurrence of goods spillage. Furthermore, Internet of Things (IoT) devices have the capability to monitor several metrics within a facility, including but not limited to temperature, humidity, switches, and voltage. The sensors have the capability to detect various occurrences, such as openings, leaks, battery charge levels, floods, and other related events within pipelines and equipment. The monitoring of metrics inside a warehouse setting is of utmost importance as distributors strive to mitigate any disruptions and inefficiencies by implementing predictive maintenance strategies.

Aggregators

Aggregators refer to platforms or systems that collect and compile various pieces of information from multiple. One further method by which organizations utilize e-commerce for investments and problems related to Internet of Things (IoT) applications is through the inclusion of aggregators in their product offers (Kucuk, 2017). The utilization of Internet of Things (IoT) applications enables organizations to optimize their reach and enhance market penetration, hence facilitating increased expenditures. However, this endeavor is not without its hurdles. Simultaneously, it facilitates enhanced trial creation and repeat purchases for firms' product offers in the context of Internet of Things (IoT) applications, as discussed by Išoraitė (2016) and Groucutt & Hopkins (2015).

Optimize Operations

In order to enhance operational efficiency and effectiveness, it is imperative to optimize operations. In light of the significant disruptions experienced this year, it is imperative for distributors to avoid the occurrence of malfunctioning machinery that could further impede the distribution process. In order to address this difficulty, distributors must prioritize routine maintenance activities and proactively address any potential issues before they escalate into major repairs or, worse yet, machinery failures. Distributors have the capability to utilize Internet of Things (IoT)-enabled sensors that are connected to essential machinery located across the distribution floor. In this manner, personnel can receive immediate automated notifications when significant metrics deviate from standard ranges or when a machinery's performance falls below average levels. In the event of an atypical temperature within a facility, the facility manager possesses the ability to delegate the task of modifying the thermostat to prevent any potential harm to the products.

Supply Chain Sourcing

The process of supply chain sourcing involves the identification, evaluation, and selection of suppliers to meet the procurement needs of an organization. In the case that a provider is unable to meet the designated delivery timeline, an automatic exploration for an alternative source may be initiated within the interconnected intelligent system (Chatterjee, 2016). Implementing this measure would effectively prevent any potential disruptions in the manufacturing schedule, customer service operations, or revenue stream.

Mitigate the Occurrence of Theft

The Internet of Things (IoT) has the potential to have a significant impact in the realm of burglary prevention. The majority of security alarms are often linked by the global system for mobile communications (GSM). However, the prevalence of GSM jammers in the market poses a significant vulnerability, allowing hackers to quickly compromise these systems. Distribution managers have the ability to mitigate the occurrence of jams by implementing alarms that are enabled by the Internet of Things (IoT) and operate on a 0G network. These alarms offer a cost-effective solution to safeguarding buildings and effectively address the issue of jamming. The 0G alarms utilize radio technology, which confers resistance to jamming, hence enhancing the reliability of alarm systems. The inclusion of this additional security measure will provide distribution managers with a sense of reassurance, as they can be confident that their items are protected.

Specialty Stores

Specialty stores, often known as niche stores, are retail establishments that focus on selling a specific category of products. It is noteworthy that organizations invest in Internet of Things (IoT) applications and face problems in doing so. Additionally, these enterprises stock their items in specialty stores (Grewal & Levy, 2021). This strategy enables the organization to achieve direct visibility among its intended market and audience, facilitating direct engagement between customers and the brand and its products or services while minimizing extraneous distractions (Kotler & Keller, 2021; Gillespie & Swan, 2021). Specialty stores are strategically situated in prominent areas, enabling firms to invest in and tackle the problems of Internet of Things (IoT) applications. This results in a greater level of market penetration and wider reach, ultimately leading to enhanced brand recognition for the products they sell (Groucutt & Hopkins, 2015; Išoraitė, 2016).

Big Data

The immediate consequence of the Internet of Things (IoT) is the increased burden placed on a company's network infrastructure. In the facilities, a considerable number of Internet of Things (IoT) devices may be present, potentially ranging from hundreds to even thousands. All of these systems gather data and require the transmission of that data to backend applications, hence necessitating a greater demand for network bandwidth. The direction of data transmission also exhibits variations, with a significant increase in east-west traffic compared to conventional applications. In addition to potentially requiring increased network capacity, there may also be a need for its expansion into previously unaddressed locations. The sensors of all Internet of Things (IoT) devices are continually collecting data. A portion of the available data can be effectively utilized for automated decision-making processes, such as the scheduling of preventive maintenance activities for equipment. Additional data can be utilized to enhance analytics, hence facilitating the decision-making process for the management team in crucial business matters. The storage capacity necessary for storing this data is expected to exceed the desired expansion limit of your data center.

Direct Sales

The concept of direct sales refers to the marketing and selling of products or services directly to consumers without the involvement of intermediaries. The investments and problems associated with Internet of Things (IoT) applications in organizations are further complemented by the presence of a proficient sales force that is equipped to engage in direct sales (Kotler & Keller, 2021). The investments and problems associated with the applications of the Internet of Things (IoT) are aimed at organizations, encompassing both business-to-consumer (B2C) and business-to-business (B2B) consumers (Chernev, 2018; Grewal & Levy, 2021). Both of these categories also employ direct marketing strategies, in which sales agents and teams directly contact the target audience and businesses to provide a comprehensive explanation of the product's characteristics and benefits (Kotler & Keller, 2021; Groucutt & Hopkins, 2015).

Supply Chain Planning

Supply chain planning refers to the process of strategically managing and optimizing the flow of goods, services, and information from the point of origin to the point of consumption. It involves the Internet of Things (IoT) has the capability to detect and monitor the demand for finished products through the utilization of embedded intelligent devices. The implementation of the Internet of Things (IoT) will facilitate the automated tracking of finished products within the supply chain, encompassing different distribution centers and sales channels. This will effectively monitor the availability of products and provide real-time insights into the current demand. In the event of unavailability of inventory, the system has the capability to assess the availability of raw materials and manufacturing capacity. This assessment enables the system to initiate an automatic production trigger to the relevant entity (Chatterjee, 2016).

The utilization of these technologies allows for the collection of data, which in turn provides comprehensive visibility of a product's journey from its origin at the producer to its final destination at the store (Chatterjee, 2016). The Internet of Things (IoT) has the capability to effectively oversee inventory management in warehouses and distribution centers through the implementation of automated inventory flow and control mechanisms, hence mitigating instances of stock shortages. The Internet of Things (IoT) is also being utilized in the identification of waste materials and the implementation of procedures aimed at reducing waste. The primary factor contributing to in-transit visibility is the utilization of cloud-based GPS and Radio Frequency Identification (RFID) technologies, which provide the acquisition of identity, position, and additional tracking data. Fleet management systems employ various technologies to reduce fuel expenses and enhance fleet efficiency through the monitoring of traffic conditions for route optimization. The utilization of GPS and RFID technologies enables the automation of shipping and delivery processes by accurately forecasting the anticipated time of arrival.

Business-to-business

Business-to-business (B2B) and direct sales are two distinct approaches to selling products or services. B2B sales involve transactions between two businesses when one business sells its offerings to another business. The team responsible for enterprise sales during field visits utilizes investments and addresses issues related to Internet of Things (IoT) applications (Sahaf, 2019; Stead & Hastings, 2018). The target audience is meticulously assessed and chosen by 'The Internet of Things (IoT) Applications: Investments and Challenges for Enterprises' in order to enable sales reps to effectively sift through extraneous information (Gillespie &

Swan, 2021; Išoraitė, 2016). The investments and problems associated with the applications of the Internet of Things (IoT) enable organizations to establish seamless and efficient communication with specific business groups (Groucutt & Hopkins, 2015; Abratt & Bendixen, 2018).

IoT Commerce

IoT Commerce must make a decision about the implementation of a distribution system, with the options being direct, indirect, or both. The process of channel design encompasses various factors, including the comprehension of the customer value proposition, the existing customer convenience points, the extent and scope of the IoT commerce product line, and the distribution systems employed by competitors (Schwaderer, 2015). IoTs Commerce has established its own direct distribution channel in order to directly engage customers. The company can choose to establish physical retail locations or exclusively engage in online sales for its whole product range. The indirect distribution system is a viable approach in the realm of IoT commerce, encompassing various channel partners such as wholesalers, retailers, logistics businesses, and distribution agencies. IoTs commerce ought to adopt a hybrid model that involves the delegation of ancillary functions, such as logistics, warehousing, and store management, to different channel partners while retaining control over the important portion of the distribution system. Enterprises strategically invest in Internet of Things (IoT) applications to proficiently handle inventory and promptly meet retailer demands, hence ensuring efficient customer relationship management and client retention. The use of the Internet of Things (IoT) in organizations has brought both investments and problems. One notable application of IoT is in the realm of inventory management, where automation has been introduced. This automation has the potential to enhance efficiency and speed while simultaneously reducing mistake rates (Park, 2020; Gillespie & Swan, 2021; Kucuk, 2017). The investments and challenges associated with Internet of Things (IoT) applications in organizations encompass the selection of economically viable transportation methods for inventory management, as well as the timely delivery of orders to both customers and retailers. The organization employs both external transportation services and internal transportation networks to guarantee punctual delivery of orders (Abratt & Bendixen, 2018; Chernev, 2018; Grewal & Levy, 2021).

Internet of Things (IoT) sensors have the capability to effectively monitor the temperature and humidity levels of perishable items during transportation, thereby ensuring adherence to optimal conditions and reducing wastage. The utilization of Internet of Things (IoT)-enabled sensors and telematics provide an opportunity to effectively monitor various aspects of vehicle operations, including performance, driver behavior, and fuel consumption. This enables organizations to enhance their fleet management practices through the implementation of optimization strategies. The utilization of Internet of Things (IoT) sensors facilitates the monitoring of product whereabouts and motion within warehouses, hence enabling organizations to enhance their warehouse management strategies and enhance operational effectiveness. The implementation of Internet of Things (IoT) technology in the context of warehouse management offers numerous advantages to the organization. The implementation of IoT technology effectively mitigates the limitations imposed by time restrictions and human errors that arise from manual product tracking processes. By employing radio frequency identification (RFID) tags and sensors on merchandise, enterprises have the capability to monitor the movement of inventory as it enters and exits their premises. The provided data is utilized by an enterprise resource planning (ERP) system to facilitate the continuous replenishment of inventory.

The Implementation of Proactive Maintenance Strategies for Assets

Internet of Things (IoT) sensors have the capability to effectively monitor the operational efficiency of various assets, including trucks, ships, and airplanes. This monitoring capability empowers managers to proactively detect and address possible maintenance concerns, thereby preventing them from escalating into significant difficulties. Furthermore, the utilization of IoT sensors facilitates the optimization of maintenance schedules, ensuring that resources are allocated efficiently.

Autonomous Cars and Drones

The Internet of Things (IoT) facilitates the ability of autonomous vehicles and drones to gather and interpret data from their surroundings, thereby empowering them to move and function independently. The following examples illustrate the application of Internet of Things (IoT) technology in supply chain and logistics operations. The Internet of Things (IoT) is playing a significant role in the transformation of logistics and supply chain management. It facilitates the achievement of real-time visibility, control, and optimization of diverse activities, leading to cost reduction, enhanced efficiency, and improved customer service. Internet of Things (IoT) devices have the potential to enhance the monitoring and visibility of commodities along the supply chain by facilitating the continuous tracking of their whereabouts, conditions, and status in real-time as they progress through various phases of the supply chain. There exist several methods by which Internet of Things (IoT) devices can enhance the monitoring and transparency of commodities across the entirety of the supply chain.

Radio Frequency Identification (RFID)

Radio frequency identification (RFID) tags are utilized to monitor the movement of commodities within the supply chain. These tags are affixed to the items and enable the tracking of their whereabouts. IoT-enabled devices have the capability to read the tags and subsequently transfer the collected data to a centralized system, facilitating real-time monitoring.

Global Positioning System (GPS)

The utilization of global positioning system (GPS) technology for tracking purposes. The utilization of GPS tracking enables the monitoring of the geographical position of items as they traverse the various stages of the supply chain. Internet of Things (IoT)-enabled devices have the capability to broadcast location data to a centralized system, hence facilitating real-time monitoring.

The Provision of Instantaneous Notifications

Internet of Things (IoT) equipped devices have the capability to transmit immediate notifications to supply chain managers and other relevant parties in the event of any complications or disruptions occurring during the transportation of goods along the supply chain. Internet of Things (IoT) devices have the capability to enhance the level of visibility and transparency within the supply chain by facilitating the tracking and monitoring of commodities. This enhanced visibility empowers supply chain managers to promptly detect and address issues and inefficiencies, hence enabling rapid and effective responses. The utilization of such devices in the Internet of Things (IoT) supply chain enables organizations to enhance operational efficiency, minimize expenses, and enhance the quality of customer service.

Benefits of IoT for Place/SCM/Distribution

The Internet of Things (IoT) possesses the capacity to significantly transform supply chain management through the provision of unparalleled levels of real-time visibility and control across the entirety of the supply chain. Internet of Things (IoT) sensors have the capability to effectively monitor and track the geographical whereabouts and overall state of commodities across the entire supply chain. This feature enables businesses to attain instantaneous visibility of their inventory, hence facilitating the optimization of inventory management, mitigating the occurrence of stockouts, and averting the issue of overstocking. The implementation of Internet of Things (IoT) devices has the potential to streamline several labor-intensive tasks within supply chain management. These tasks include but are not limited to monitoring inventory levels and organizing maintenance schedules. This has the potential to result in substantial financial savings and enhanced operational effectiveness.

Channel management involves the administration of different power centers within the delivery system, with a focus on effectively managing these centers in accordance with the negotiating power possessed by each participant in the value chain. The topic of interest is the per-unit cost of stocking. In the event of elevated costs, the implementation of IoT commerce necessitates the involvement of channel partners who possess the ability to collectively contribute resources. Alternatively, IoT commerce has the capability to independently perform the necessary procedures. Customers are inclined to engage in search behavior and travel in order to make a purchase. If the level of consumer willingness is high, it indicates that the company has a robust brand awareness and brand loyalty. The implementation of Internet of Things (IoT) technology in commerce has the potential to create advantageous channel policies in relation to channel partners. The necessity of market development requirements arises. Market development is considered to be a highly significant function of a channel. If the commerce of the Internet of Things (IoT) requires increased efforts in market expansion, it would be prudent to incorporate channel partners who possess the knowledge and expertise to expand into untapped regions. The Internet of Things (IoT) facilitates the monitoring of a product across its entire supply chain, encompassing the period from its departure from the manufacturer's production line to its arrival at the customer's location. The Internet of Things (IoT) enables businesses to receive timely notifications regarding detained shipments and offers up-to-date information on customer deliveries. The Internet of Things (IoT) facilitates the collection of a larger volume of data, hence enhancing the comprehension of client behaviors and requirements. This observation has the potential to contribute to the development of an improved customer experience at all points of contact, encompassing activities such as pre-sale browsing and purchases, as well as post-sales engagements. Business enterprises possess the capability to notify their clientele in instances where their inventory levels for particular items are dwindling, when the warranty period for a product is nearing its conclusion, or when a frequently purchased item is being offered at a discounted price. Customers highly value the individualized attention and effectiveness that they derive from these updates.

In contrast, closed systems exhibit reduced speed and increased complexity in terms of accessibility. Cloud-based Internet of Things (IoT) technologies facilitate the provision of relevant data to all stakeholders involved in the supply chain lifecycle, enabling prompt resolution of any potential issues that may develop during the process. These technologies are additionally bolstered by web and mobile applications that cater to a diverse array of users, including workers, managers, and consumers. These users have the ability to employ these tools in various circumstances. The investments and challenges associated with the applications of the Internet of Things (IoT) for organizations. Licensed outlets provide consumers with the opportunity to partake in the diverse range of products offered by the company. Licensed stores provide a means of mitigating the potential risks associated with financial and physical investments in the Internet of Things (IoT) applications, particularly for firms operating in volatile markets. Licensed establishments have also provided organizations with significant commercial growth opportunities and facilitated quick market expansion and penetration through investments in Internet of Things (IoT) applications. These developments, however, come with their own set of hurdles. Licensed stores have provided valuable insights into local consumers and cultures, hence enhancing the understanding of Internet of Things (IoT) applications' investments and issues for organizations. Licensed stores and shops strategically promote the sales of items by investments in Internet of Things (IoT) applications, while also addressing the issues faced by enterprises. This is achieved by matching these investments with the cultural values prevalent in the local community. Licensed stores also contribute to the facilitation of Internet of Things (IoT) applications expenditures and problems for organizations by enabling them to localize their product offerings, hence enhancing brand equity and brand image.

The Internet of Things (IoT) facilitates the ability of merchants and supply chain managers to make informed decisions regarding the procurement of products. This is achieved through the utilization of accurate data on the turnover of commodities, enabling them to estimate the optimal quantity of each commodity to be purchased. The utilization of the Internet of Things (IoT) in enhancing asset monitoring, shipping, and navigation also serves to mitigate the impact of human error. The enhancement of overall supply chain performance is facilitated by the utilization of route-planning applications and Internet of Things (IoT) monitoring systems. The utilization of these technologies can lead to expedited decision-making, mitigation of potential risks, and enhanced overall productivity. The Internet of Things (IoT) facilitates the acquisition of dependable and up-to-date data, enabling individuals and organizations to make better-informed decisions that align with their strategic objectives and enhance their prospects for future achievements. The acquisition of knowledge is a potent force, thereby highlighting the significance of the Internet of Things (IoT) in establishing a comprehensive omnichannel enterprise. The organization oversees the operation of stores managed by the Internet of Things (IoT) applications, addressing the investments and issues faced by enterprises across various markets. Company-operated stores provide organizations with increased control over operations, store layout, and design, hence presenting opportunities and problems in the realm of

Internet of Things (IoT) applications. The investments and problems associated with Internet of Things (IoT) applications in organizations are closely intertwined with consumer interactions and the collection of significant information on consumer behavior and feedback through company-operated storefronts. The presence of company-operated stores presents organizations with opportunities and problems in terms of their investments and decision-making surrounding the stocking of various product items within the context of Internet of Things (IoT) applications. Internet of Things (IoT) sensors have the capability to monitor the operational state of machinery and equipment, so enabling enterprises to anticipate and forecast maintenance needs. Implementing this strategy can effectively mitigate equipment failures and minimize operational disruptions, hence resulting in enhanced efficiency and productivity. The utilization of real-time data derived from Internet of Things (IoT) sensors can significantly enhance firms' ability to make well-informed decisions pertaining to inventory management, production planning, and logistics. This phenomenon has the potential to enhance supply chain performance and bolster customer happiness. The utilization of Internet of Things (IoT) sensors has the potential to facilitate the tracking and monitoring of commodities across the entirety of the supply chain. This capability can effectively mitigate the risk of spoiling and minimize wastage. In general, the advantages of the Internet of Things (IoT) in the context of supply chain management are substantial, and organizations that use this technology are expected to attain a competitive edge within the market. Internet of Things (IoT) equipped sensors have the capability to monitor inventory levels in real time, hence offering immediate visibility into stock levels. This facilitates firms in enhancing their inventory management procedures through optimization. The utilization of Internet of Things (IoT) sensors has the capability to facilitate the monitoring of supplier performance, hence allowing firms to effectively identify possible bottlenecks and optimize their supply chain networks.

The utilization of the Internet of Things (IoT) has the potential to facilitate the monitoring and management of various assets. In contemporary business practices, managers are no longer reliant on manual data entry or traditional inventory devices for the purpose of asset management. Rather, the advent of software technology has enabled the automation of this process. The utilization of interconnected technology, encompassing sensors, RFID tags, beacons, and smart materials, facilitates the expeditious retrieval of vital data pertaining to every shipment within the supply chain. This includes pertinent details regarding the package's contents, storage guidelines, and other relevant information. Enterprises have made significant expenditures in the development of operational websites for online order placement and order tracking within the realm of the Internet of Things (IoT) applications. The use of Internet of Things (IoT) applications presents both investment opportunities and challenges for organizations.

Additionally, enterprises are leveraging social media portals to facilitate sales, wherein orders are received through direct messages, and a mini-shop model is employed. In addition to distributing its items through online marketplaces like Amazon and eBay, the company also collaborates with smaller local online shops. The utilization of online platforms for retail purposes, particularly through the Internet, has significantly contributed to the augmentation of sales for various businesses. The proliferation of Internet of Things (IoT) applications has led to increasing investments and problems for organizations while simultaneously enhancing the accessibility of IoT items for consumers.

Currently, the implementation of Internet of Things (IoT)-enabled supply chain management systems is widely regarded as a prominent advancement in warehouse technology. The implementation of warehouse procedures leads to enhanced efficiency, resulting in greater accuracy in inventory management and enhanced personnel safety. On-site employees may efficiently locate things and promptly navigate to the appropriate aisle for a certain product, facilitated by the utilization of real-time location trackers. The Internet of Things (IoT) enables the seamless management of operations and facilitates the delivery of superior outcomes that would otherwise be unachievable. Furthermore, the Internet of Things (IoT) serves as a crucial component in the progression toward achieving full warehouse automation, minimizing the need for human intervention, particularly when combined with artificial intelligence (AI). Firms face both investments and obstacles when it comes to the applications of the Internet of Things (IoT). Additionally, these firms distribute their products in supermarkets and hypermarkets nationwide. Enterprises primarily focus their efforts and encounter obstacles in several applications of the Internet of Things (IoT), particularly in the context of groups of consumers that engage in shopping activities at supermarkets and hypermarkets. The strategic positioning of products in supermarkets and hypermarkets can enhance cost efficiency.

In the context of offshore locations, firms engage in investments and encounter obstacles related to the implementation of Internet of Things (IoT) applications. These enterprises also rely on partner agents to facilitate the deployment of their products. The partner agents undergo assessment and evaluation based on their strategic compatibility and reliability. Enterprises engage in investments and encounter obstacles while implementing applications related to the Internet of Things (IoT). These applications involve establishing contracts with partner agents in various countries and marketplaces to facilitate the placement of their products. The primary objectives of such contracts are to assure quality control and establish favorable terms for negotiation. The utilization of remote monitoring technology enables the observation of equipment, containers, pallets, or packages in order to assess the performance of said equipment or to watch the movement of products across the whole supply chain. The implementation of tracking and tracing systems enables customers to consistently monitor the precise location, condition, and potential deviations from the intended route of their items. The monitoring of physical assets is essential in order to ascertain their optimal functionality or anticipate the need for maintenance in the near future. The objective of warehouse inventory management is to minimize instances of out-o--stock situations and to obtain valuable insights into client purchasing behaviors. It is imperative to prevent the spoilage of perishable food items that require transportation in temperature-controlled vehicles. The objective is to continuously monitor the assets of the warehouse equipment in real time in order to ascertain instances of excessive use or periods of idleness, hence enabling the identification of opportunities for the redeployment of assets to alternative tasks. The Internet of Things (IoT) facilitates the provision of real-time data pertaining to the position of the product and its transportation environment. Once the product has been inadvertently carried in the wrong way, you will receive prompt notification and will have the capability to monitor the progress of both finished goods and raw materials as they approach their destination. The utilization of Internet of Things (IoT) technology enables the monitoring of both raw and finished materials, along with their respective attributes, such as quantity, classification, and geographical information, throughout the entire life cycle, starting from a tier-n supplier and concluding with the end consumer. This implementation is anticipated to yield favorable effects on inventory management, sourcing strategies, and logistics expenses.

Implications

The utilization of Internet of Things (IoT) devices by leaders plays a pivotal role in the implementation of transportation chain strategies. The utilization of Internet of Things (IoT) technology for the purpose of precise and transparent shipment monitoring is of great relevance to end users. Authenticity monitoring for critical and highly valuable items is a matter of interest for business users and supply chain partners. Transparency regarding distribution systems, network use, and monitoring of assets is crucial for logistics organizations in order to enhance operational efficiency through optimization. The utilization of IoT is imperative in the development of a comprehensive and cohesive controller that facilitates the identification of the appropriate product at the optimal moment, in the correct location, with the precise quantity and condition, and at a suitable cost.

CONCLUSION

In conclusion, it can be inferred that the information provided supports the notion the Internet of Things (IoT) is poised to become the next technological revolution.

The implementation of advanced distribution, materials handling equipment, and sensors in warehouses has the potential to significantly transform operations, resulting in increased efficiency, cost-effectiveness, and productivity. The integration of the Internet of Things (IoT) into warehouse operations encompasses the real-time monitoring of equipment, goods, pallets, and personnel, as well as the measurement of their performance. By applying analytics to the collected data, potential areas for enhancement can be identified. The manual handling of inventory can be minimized. The optimization of individuals and equipment is possible. Enhancing safety and anticipating equipment malfunctions through the monitoring of both equipment and personnel has the potential to enhance asset utilization.

REFERENCES

Abratt, R., Bendixen, M. (2018). *Strategic marketing: Concepts and cases.* New York, United States: Routledge.
[http://dx.doi.org/10.4324/9780429489327]

Atzori, L., Iera, A., Morabito, G. (2017). Understanding the Internet of Things: definition, potentials, and societal role of a fast evolving paradigm. *Ad Hoc Netw, 56*, 122-140.
[http://dx.doi.org/10.1016/j.adhoc.2016.12.004]

Baines, P., Fill, C., Rosengren, S. (2017). *Marketing.* New York, United States: Oxford University Press.

Carniel, A. (2022). The ultimate guide to marketing mix: 4Ps, 7Ps, 8Ps, 4Cs, 7Cs. Available from: https://www.albertocarniel.com/post/marketing-mix.

Chatterjee, R. (2016). Benefits of Internet of Things (IoT) over Supply Chain and Logistics Industry. Available from: https://www.linkedin.com/pulse/benefits-internet-things-iot-over-supply-chain-rahul-chatterjee.

Chernev, A. (2018). *Strategic marketing management.* Berlin/Heidelberg, Germany: Cerebellum Press.

Gillespie, K., Swan, K. (2021). *Global marketing.* New York, United States: Routledge.
[http://dx.doi.org/10.4324/9781003141709]

Grewal, D., Levy, M. (2021). *M: marketing.* New York, United States: McGraw-Hill Education.

Groucutt, J., Hopkins, C. (2015). *Marketing.* London: Macmillan International Higher Education.

Iacobucci, D. (2021). *Marketing management.* Boston, Massachusetts, United States: Cengage Learning.

Išoraitė, M. (2016). Marketing mix theoretical aspects. *International Journal of Research - GRANTHAALAYAH, 4*(6), 25-37.
[http://dx.doi.org/10.29121/granthaalayah.v4.i6.2016.2633]

Joghee, S. (2021). Retracted article: Internet of things-assisted e-marketing and distribution framework. *Soft Comput, 25*(18), 12291-12303.
[http://dx.doi.org/10.1007/s00500-021-05920-0]

Kabalci, Y., Kabalci, E., Padmanaban, S., Holm-Nielsen, J.B., Blaabjerg, F. (2019). Internet of Things Applications as Energy Internet in Smart Grids and Smart Environments. *Electronics (Basel), 8*(9), 972.
[http://dx.doi.org/10.3390/electronics8090972]

Khan, M. (2014). The concept of marketing mix and its elements. *Int. J. Inf. Bus. Manag, 6*(2), 95-107.

Kotler, P., Keller, K. (2021). *Marketing Management (15th global edition).* London, United Kingdom: Pearson Education Limited.

Kucuk, S. (2017). Marketing and Marketing Mix. *Visualizing Marketing* (pp. 3-7). London, United Kingdom: Palgrave Macmillan.
[http://dx.doi.org/10.1007/978-3-319-48027-5_2]

Hossein Motlagh, N., Mohammadrezaei, M., Hunt, J., Zakeri, B. (2020). Internet of Things (IoT) and the energy sector. *Energies, 13*(2), 494.
[http://dx.doi.org/10.3390/en13020494]

Park, S. (2020). Marketing management (Vol. 3). Retrieved June 2022. Available from: https://books.google.com.pk/books/about/Marketing_Management.html?id=p6v7DwAAQBAJ&redir_esc=y.

Pogorelova, E.V., Yakhneeva, I.V., Agafonovaa, A.N., Prokubovskaya, A.O. (2016). Marketing Mix for E-commerce. *Int. J. Environ. Sci. Educ, 11*(14), 6744-6759.

Sahaf, A. (2019). *Strategic marketing: Making decisions for strategic advantage.* New Delhi, India: PHI Learning Pvt. Ltd..

Stead, M., Hastings, G. (2018). Advertising in the social marketing mix: getting the balance right. *Social Marketing* (pp. 29-43). London, England: Psychology Press.
[http://dx.doi.org/10.4324/9781315805795-3]

Schwaderer, C. (2015). The distribution of things: IoT, M2M, and software distribution. Available from: https://embeddedcomputing.com/technology/iot/the-distribution-of-things-iot-m2m-and-s-ftware-distribution-2.

Wu, Y.L., Li, E.Y. (2018). Marketing mix, customer value, and customer loyalty in social commerce. *Internet Res, 28*(1), 74-104.
[http://dx.doi.org/10.1108/IntR-08-2016-0250]

CHAPTER 7

Internet of Things in Marketing: The Customer Experience

Salifu Shani[1,*], **Mohammed Majeed**[2], **Parag Shukla**[3] and **Sofia Devi Shamurailatpam**[4]

[1] *Chicago School of Professional Psychology, Chicago, United State*

[2] *Department of Marketing, Tamale Technical University, Tamale, Ghana*

[3] *Department of Commerce and Business Management, The Maharaja Sayajirao University of Baroda, Gujarat, India*

[4] *Department of Banking and Insurance, The Maharaja Sayajirao University of Baroda, Gujarat, India*

Abstract: Undoubtedly, the Internet of Things (IoT) possesses the capacity to enhance customer experiences. The exponential growth of technology has had a profound influence on various aspects of enterprises. In addition, the Internet of Things (IoT) facilitates the exchange of data, facilitates the control of inventory, enhances security measures, and contributes to heightened levels of efficiency and production. The purpose of the chapter is to review the literature to understand how IoT is used in marketing to affect customer experience. IoT has the capability to revolutionize current business models by facilitating novel interactions and establishing new partnerships between organizations and their customers. Adopting the end-customer standpoint offers guidance and illuminates potential avenues for the creation of services that are embraced and financially supported by both enterprises and customers. This will facilitate the development of novel and inventive services, thereby fundamentally transforming operational practices across several sectors in the future. The contemporary customer base is undergoing a transformation, wherein they are increasingly accustomed to immediate accessibility. Consequently, they now anticipate that their consumption and purchasing encounters will be characterized by immediacy, distinctiveness, and emotional resonance. Therefore, it is imperative for organizations to gain a comprehensive understanding of the fundamental shifts in consumer habits in order to develop appropriate and pleasurable customer experiences across both online and offline channels. In the preceding study, the focus was on the emergence of a novel type of consumer, with particular attention given to the evolution of their social standing, requirements, and their involvement in the brand or company's interactions.

Keywords: Customer, Experience, Internet of Things, Internet, Technology.

---

[*] **Corresponding author Salifu Shani:** Chicago School of Professional Psychology, Chicago, United State;
E-mail: ssalifu@thechicagoschool.edu

INTRODUCTION

According to Eguillor (2018), it was projected that by the year 2020, the global quantity of Internet-connected devices would approach approximately 50 billion. The pervasive presence of newly interconnected items serves as a testament to the significant scale of this technological phenomenon, exemplified by the Internet of Things (IoT), which spans various industries, sectors, and geographical locations worldwide. With the increasing prevalence of smart and online interaction capabilities being integrated into a wide range of objects, the potential applications become limitless. The Internet of Things (IoT) is a significant technological development with the potential to exert a lasting influence on the social landscape in the foreseeable future. The continuous expansion of emerging interconnected gadgets presents several opportunities across various industries while also introducing a novel framework for marketing management and client interactions (Eguillor, 2018). The optimization of customer service can be achieved by the utilization of real-time information offered by these technologies. In the realm of marketing and advertising, this phenomenon results in the emergence of novel prospects for engagement. The concept of the Internet of Things (IoT) refers to a network of numerous physical objects or entities, commonly referred to as "things", which are equipped with software, sensors, and various other technologies. These objects are capable of communicating and exchanging data with other systems and devices through the internet. The Internet of Things (IoT) refers to a network of interconnected mechanical and digital devices, computing systems, and objects. The transmission of data through a network can occur without the need for direct interaction between humans and computers or between humans themselves. In the contemporary business landscape, the integration of the Internet of Things (IoT) and automation technologies presents a multitude of opportunities for enhancing consumer experiences. Enterprise process automation enables organizations to establish comprehensive workflows, thereby expediting the execution of repeated tasks that would otherwise demand the attention of essential personnel. The implementation of automation techniques enables professionals to allocate a greater portion of their efforts towards the creation of exceptional customer experiences while reducing the time spent on mundane activities such as data entry. Kwiatkowska (2014) posits that the Internet is undergoing a transformation from a network primarily comprised of interconnected computers to a network encompassing diverse devices such as autos, cellphones, household appliances, and toys. These devices remain consistently connected, engaging in communication and information exchange with one another. This facilitates the establishment of a continuous flow of data regarding how a consumer utilizes specific products over the course of their life cycles. Furthermore, the Internet of Things (IoT) presents a substantial capacity for innovation and enables marketers to develop novel strategies for attaining a competitive edge. Furthermore, it aids organizations in the endeavor of effectively overseeing customer experience throughout their interactions with a company, brand, or product, resulting in heightened customer contentment and improved business outcomes.

The Internet of Things has a profound influence on all industries and facets of our daily existence. This technique warrants significant study due to several compelling justifications. The primary advantages of the Internet of Things (IoT) encompass the interconnection of small-scale components that are integral to our everyday routines, facilitating the exchange of data and enabling the automation of various processes. A plethora of applications are currently accessible to fulfill the needs of consumers, business enterprises, and infrastructural requirements. This essay will primarily concentrate on the Internet of Things (IoT) and customer experience management, considering their significant potential in several domains. The Internet of Things (IoT) is a technology that is neither novel, overblown, nor remote. The existing presence of this phenomenon is pervasive and is expected to undergo further advancements and utilization. Hence, the chapter looks at the IoT to affect customer experience.

LITERATURE

CX

Customer experience management is a matter of concern for both service companies and customers alike. Regrettably, it is prevalent for this service to exhibit a significantly substandard degree of quality. In contemporary times, adherence to modern methodologies, integration of cutting-edge technologies, and provision of exemplary customer service are crucial for the success of a corporation. The competition is highly intense, and the consequences of failure are significant. The correlation between the quality of a customer experience plan and the likelihood of achieving success is positive. The Internet of Things (IoT) holds a distinct position within the various methods employed to enhance the consumer experience. The concept of customer experience encompasses the various interactions that occur between a customer and an organization or product. These interactions are characterized by their unique nature and can encompass logical, sentimental, sensorial, tangible, and even spiritual elements (Gentile, Spiller, & Noci, 2007). Alternatively, customer experience can be understood as a multifaceted concept that encompasses the cognitive, affective, behavioral, physical, and psychological reactions of customers to the products and services a business provides throughout their purchasing journey (Lemon & Verhoef, 2016). According to Sudolska (2011), the customer experience encompasses the entirety of impressions formed as a consequence of all interactions between customers and a company, including engagements with its products, staff, services, self-service technology, and the associated informational messages. The customer experience development process encompasses various stages, namely awareness, discovery, attraction, engagement, purchase, use, nurturing, and advocacy (Kocher, 2017). The ultimate outcome of customer experience pertains to the perceptions and emotions that customers hold towards a company or brand, as well as the level of connection established between them (Kocher, 2017).

Internet of Things

The notion of the Internet of Things (IoT) was first recognized in 1999 as a means to facilitate the utilization of radio frequency identification (RFID) technology and associated computing devices (Ray, 2018). The array of devices encompasses a variety of technological instruments, including computers, cellphones, wireless sensor networks, home and building automation systems, manufacturing tools, software applications, and smart appliances (Lo & Campos, 2018). The utilization of the Internet of Things (IoT) enables individuals and entities to obtain a diverse range of advantages through the gathering, analysis, and transmission of data. For example, the utilization of Internet of Things (IoT) devices enables the potential for electronic methods to detect, manage, and even avoid illnesses (Vermesan & Friess, 2014). Furthermore, it is feasible to combine and merge various consumer devices into a unified Internet of Things (IoT) system, so augmenting the efficacy of power utilization. Within the field of marketing, the utilization of intelligent appliances that are connected to the Internet of Things (IoT) enables the monitoring of product supply. This monitoring process subsequently facilitates the provision of suggestions to owners pertaining to new purchases, offers, and emerging trends. According to Moradi (2021), a significant increase in the number of Internet of Things (IoT) devices is anticipated, with projections suggesting that it might reach 30 billion by the year 2020. This forecast aligns with the predictions made by several researchers and IT specialists. The Internet of Things (IoT) refers to the interconnectedness of digital devices, which offers numerous possibilities for brands to effectively communicate with their customers by delivering appropriate messages at the appropriate moment using the appropriate device. In contemporary business sectors, intensifying competition among firms necessitates the adoption of diverse strategies to attain a competitive edge. One strategy that might be employed is the customization of services to meet individual needs. All corporations endeavor to enhance their customer service. Ultimately, this phenomenon serves as a catalyst for increased customer demand for services that are tailored to individual preferences and needs. The utilization of the Internet of Things (IoT) has the potential to assist businesses in fulfilling client demands for tailored and individualized services. The utilization of the Internet of Things (IoT) and Big Data has shown to be crucial in enhancing customer service. However, the storage and collection of substantial volumes of data pose significant challenges. Fortunately, the application of Big Data analytics offers a viable solution to address these challenges. In the absence of the Internet of Things, managing client data might also provide challenges. For instance, in the scenario where a consumer makes a purchase from an e-commerce platform, they subsequently receive an electronic communication with further product recommendations that may not align with their preferences or needs. In the present era, corporations have the ability to employ the Internet of Things (IoT) to effectively target their product listings toward clients by leveraging real-life circumstances. In instances where a customer makes a purchase, it is common for a complementary product or accessory to be recommended alongside the original one. The extent of interactions between the corporation and its clients was restricted solely to the point of sale. In order to comprehend client demands and behavior, it is imperative for businesses to collect information through customer reviews, surveys, and complaints. However, in the present scenario, enterprises equipped with Internet of Things (IoT) devices have the capability to get instantaneous data from their clientele and actively interact with them. Through the examination of gathered data, organizations have the ability to predict and effectively address the needs and desires of their clientele. Sales teams have the ability to utilize data in order to comprehend and effectively address consumer requirements during the process of making sales.

INTERNET OF THINGS IMPACTING ON CUSTOMER EXPERIENCE

Optimized Usage of the Product

The Internet of Things (IoT) enables organizations to gather substantial amounts of data. The process of data collection can assist organizations in optimizing their products. According to Reji (2020), enterprises have the potential to enhance the entire value of a product by leveraging the data they acquire regarding its usage. Companies have the ability to utilize Internet of Things (IoT) data in order to identify and assess the performance of their products. Based on the aforementioned, organizations have the ability to identify potential concerns and enhance product development. Organizations have the capability to utilize this technology to notify their clientele regarding the operational status and discern when repair activities would be necessary. This can assist the organization in enhancing the efficiency of product processes, hence benefiting customers. According to Anand (2023), the enhancement of performance and the cultivation of stronger relationships are observed as positive outcomes.

Enhanced Client Service

Enhancing customer service is a vital consideration within the very competitive corporate landscape in order to achieve success. The utilization of the Internet of Things has the potential to facilitate the provision of satisfactory customer service in this particular scenario. The failure of essential tools or equipment can be identified as a significant factor impeding the provision of enhanced customer care (Anand, 2023). Nevertheless, with the utilization of the Internet of Things (IoT)-connected devices and sensors, it is possible to anticipate potential problems that may pose a threat to your equipment. This proactive approach enables the reception of real-time alerts in the event of a malfunction, hence facilitating the reduction of downtime.

Enhancing the Quality of Products and Services

Organizations are also leveraging the Internet of Things (IoT) to develop novel products and services (Reji, 2020). The data acquired by a corporation through product consumption can be leveraged to facilitate the development of novel products. The firm has the capability to delineate the specific components of its items that are amenable to renewal. Furthermore, by utilizing the collected analytics, organizations can implement suitable measures to enhance the quality of customer services. The Internet of Things (IoT) facilitates the seamless interchange of information and the effortless collection of data, thereby providing enterprises with a very convenient and efficient means of operation (Reji, 2020). The cohesive digital environment facilitates the optimization of workers' productivity by equipping them with the necessary resources and expertise for achieving their goals. The Internet of Things (IoT) facilitates the prompt identification of faults by teams through real-time monitoring of systems. The utilization of IoT technology enables teams to adopt a proactive approach rather than a reactive one, hence enhancing productivity and efficiency.

Enhanced Security

While the Internet offers several benefits for enterprises, it also poses various threats. Security is one of the prevailing concerns. The utilization of the internet by malicious actors to unlawfully acquire data poses significant risks to corporations and other entities. It is imperative for businesses to ensure the security and restricted accessibility of their data to prevent unauthorized individuals from gaining access. According to Anand (2023), the Internet of Things (IoT) has the potential to provide enhanced security measures for safeguarding personal information. This can be achieved by the utilization of specialized networks, specific security protocols, or the incorporation of security modules into IoT systems. Cybercriminals are employing modern technology in an attempt to outsmart businesses.

IoT for Quality

Internet of Things (IoT) devices have the capability to monitor and record customer impressions, analyze this data, and afterward provide the organization with informed insights and conclusions derived from these impressions. According to Belov (2018), the Internet of Things (IoT) system possesses knowledge of the online purchases performed by clients, as well as the collection of their ratings and feedback. Comprehensive insights into client perceptions of products or services enable firms to prioritize salient elements and enhance the overall quality of their offerings in subsequent iterations.

Sales Automation

The optimization of the checkout processes is also a potential area for improvement. Consider the following scenario: an individual visits a physical retail establishment, selects the desired merchandise, and promptly exits the premises to engage in a social activity such as enjoying a cup of coffee with companions. In the meantime, the sensors autonomously identify the barcodes, conduct scans, and deduct the corresponding expenses from the linked bank account. The degree of efficiency provided is quite high. Furthermore, this innovation not only signifies a substantial enhancement in user experience but also serves as a highly efficient means for the proprietor of the establishment to economize (Belov, 2018). The implementation of IoT technology in business operations has the potential to reduce expenses related to labor and enable organizations to concentrate their efforts on the advancement of their core business activities and service offerings.

Timely and Pertinent Offerings

Machine learning has the potential to enhance the efficacy of specific advertising, but when combined with the Internet of Things (IoT), it reaches a heightened level of effectiveness. By leveraging interconnected products and services, enterprises have the capability to monitor real-time usage data, enabling them to gain insights into the specific details of how, when, and where their customers engage with their offerings. According to Ramirez (2023), the utilization of this technology enhances the capacity to tailor offerings to meet the specific demands and interests of customers in real time.

Personalization

The concept of personalization refers to the customization or tailoring of products and services, or simultaneously, the Internet of Things (IoT) system has the capability to employ an individualized approach for each customer. This technology has the potential to enable entrepreneurs to prioritize customer-centric strategies and effectively cater to their unique needs. The system analyzes the consumer experience. According to Belov (2018), this system monitors and analyzes the everyday activities of clients, enabling it to make informed decisions regarding communication strategies. Enhanced engagement, in turn, will foster a more favorable relationship between the organization and the client. The Internet of Things (IoT) is also utilized to enhance communication. The utilization of Internet of Things (IoT) technology encompasses various aspects of corporate operations, including operational management and customer behavior analysis. This enables the generation of significant data that holds relevance for businesses. By leveraging the acquired insights, organizations may effectively tailor their communication strategies to individual clients, hence enhancing customer satisfaction. The sensors embedded in items have the capability to transmit data back to the organization, providing valuable insights into usage trends.

Enhancing the Quality of In-store Encounters

The implementation of IoT connectivity in the retail industry has facilitated a more streamlined process for customers to acquire desired products, thus leading to enhanced profitability for retailers. Organizations have the ability to gather and evaluate data pertaining to the performance of their products as well as the purchasing patterns of consumers. Additionally, they can modify and optimize their physical retail establishments in order to enhance their revenue generation capabilities (Ramirez, 2023). For example, merchants have the ability to acquire visual heat maps by utilizing in-store Bluetooth beacons. These heat maps provide insights into the movement patterns of consumers within a store, which are determined by the activation of their phones' WiFi signals. According to Ramirez (2023), the utilization of movement patterns enables businesses to effectively identify regions with high foot traffic, hence facilitating strategic placement of popular products.

The Prompt and Efficient Resolution of Issues

Connected services facilitate a bilateral exchange of information between customers and businesses, hence offering expedited means to address and mitigate difficulties. By continuously observing the operational patterns of Internet of Things (IoT) devices, organizations have the capability to actively monitor their performance, promptly identify and rectify any issues that arise, and, in certain cases, address these concerns even before they become apparent to the end-user (Ramirez, 2023). The presence of wireless networking facilitates the expeditious and economical updating of items and software. For instance, automobile manufacturers are employing cellular networks to facilitate "over-the-air" updates to their interconnected vehicles in order to adhere to evolving road safety requirements (Belov, 2018).

IoT can Effectively Enhance Consumer Loyalty

As the Internet of Things (IoT) continues to advance, there will be a corresponding evolution in customer expectations and demands. According to Ramirez (2023), organizations that possess technology capable of addressing a greater number of problems and fulfilling a wider range of requirements will emerge as the ultimate beneficiaries in the realm of connected products and services.

The market for home automation, sometimes known as "smart homes", was expected to reach a value of $150 billion by the year 2020. Customers have the ability to remotely regulate several aspects of their environment, such as lighting, heating, and security. However, there is already a growing demand for further control and authority. This entails making decisions, such as utilizing energy at periods of lower cost or enabling intelligent devices to identify the optimal moment for activation. In addition, consumers express a need for optimal integration and compatibility among their various interconnected technological devices. The focus will shift from their residence to their Internet of Things (IoT) lifestyle.

The Provision of Outstanding Customer Support Services

The Internet of Things (IoT) assumes a crucial function in facilitating the development of a favorable consumer experience. Controlling equipment for issues has the potential to enhance customer happiness. Under some conditions, Internet of Things (IoT) sensors have the potential to predict and anticipate issues prior to their actual occurrence. The Internet of Things (IoT) device has the capability to transmit a notification to an engineer, notifying them of a potential issue. This enables the engineer to address the problem and perform necessary repairs prior to any occurrence of downtime.

Advertisements

Consumers perceive online advertisements as acceptable, provided that they do not disrupt their enjoyable browsing experience. It might be argued that a significant proportion of web advertisements are perceived as bothersome and lacking relevance. According to Belov (2018), the presence of such factors adversely affects the user experience, leading to instances where users may choose to close the webpage or power off their laptops. The implementation of an Internet of Things (IoT) strategy enables businesses to gain valuable insights into the preferences and dislikes of their prospective customers. This entails the absence of intrusive or confrontational advertisements on web pages, as well as the absence of interrupted transactions. Instead, only pertinent information is presented in a suitable location and at the proper time. Consumers generally see online advertisements favorably, provided that they do not disrupt or detract from their overall delightful browsing experience. It might be argued that a significant proportion of online advertisements are invasive and lack meaningful content. The aforementioned issue negatively impacts the overall user experience, leading to instances where users may opt to close the website or power down their laptops. Retailers can effectively gather information about the preferences and dislikes of their potential customers through the implementation of the Internet of Things strategy (Anand, 2023). This encompasses the absence of obtrusive or aggressive advertisements on web pages, the prevention of disrupted sales, and the provision of timely distribution of relevant information within the appropriate context.

Monitor the Movement of the Supply Chain

According to Britt (2021), the implementation of Internet of Things (IoT) technology has facilitated enhanced visibility for customers in terms of tracking the whereabouts of their orders and monitoring their progression across the supply chain. In order to enhance package tracking capabilities and improve customer satisfaction, rival enterprises have embraced novel technologies and included more devices in their operational processes. Logistics enterprises deploy Internet of Things (IoT) sensors on shipping containers to facilitate transportation operations with less human interaction while simultaneously ensuring continuous monitoring of several container attributes, including temperature, lighting, and humidity levels. Smart containers provide logistics firms with the capability to enhance the security and protection of perishable goods such as food, medications, and flowers. Additionally, they offer more accurate monitoring of the opening and closing of container doors, among other functionalities. According to Britt (2021), both the supplier and the end-user possess the ability to ascertain whether the transportation regime has been adhered to. One of the benefits of IoT data is its ability to facilitate the resolution of disputes pertaining to the substandard quality of goods that have been delivered.

The implementation of Internet of Things (IoT) technology in route management facilitates enhanced capabilities in the planning and control of shipment and delivery schedules. According to Britt (2021), the utilization of tracking equipment such as the Global Navigation Satellite System (GNSS) and dispatcher software enables the prompt identification of time delays, prevention of vehicle breakdowns, and monitoring of road accidents and impediments such as landslides and fallen trees.

Accelerated Legal Claims

Internet of Things (IoT) systems enable legal professionals to expediently and effectively collect data. According to Britt (2021), the utilization of mobile phones, GPS trackers, and smart watches enables the instantaneous transmission of data, affording legal professionals increased influence in time-critical legal matters.

Improving Business Continuity

The utilization of Internet of Things (IoT) machinery and devices enables enterprises to maintain uninterrupted operations on their production and assembly lines. According to Britt (2021), self-aware assets have the potential to independently request service, procure replacement components, and provide data on usage patterns. This data can subsequently be utilized in prediction-based models to anticipate repair requirements, hence leading to increased operational efficiency and enhanced reliability of the assets.

Trustworthy

The concept of trustworthy relationships refers to interpersonal connections characterized by reliability, dependability, and integrity. Such relationships are built on mutual trust. The phenomenon of internet fraud is not a recent development. In contemporary times, with the diligent efforts of IoT to safeguard consumers' personal data, individuals utilizing the Internet may experience heightened levels of comfort and security in their online purchasing endeavors. Nevertheless, individuals often exhibit a strong inclination to remain loyal to a certain brand, hence obviating the need to transition to an alternative online retailer and divulge personal information to unfamiliar entities (Belov, 2018). The establishment of a seamless contact between enterprises and customers, wherein the former possesses a comprehensive understanding of the latter's desires, has the potential to foster a durable and dependable partnership. This partnership, characterized by trust and reliability, has the capacity to last over an extended period of time.

IoT-enabled Devices

Another example of an Internet of Things (IoT)-enabled device is digital screens and intuitive touch screens. These strategies contribute to the enhancement of in-store advertisements and the promotion of client involvement. The Internet of Things (IoT) sensors are capable of gathering data and delivering immediate updates regarding discounts, offers, and general marketing activities across various sections of the business.

Real-Time Data

The concept of real-time data refers to the collection and analysis of information that is continuously updated and available for immediate use. The utilization of the Internet of Things (IoT) enables firms to access crucial and up-to-date data, which in turn aids in the formulation of strategic initiatives. According to Anand (2023), the implementation of IoT technology enables firms to efficiently manage unit functions and monitor product tracking in real time. This capability empowers firms to enhance their service offerings to potential clients. In addition, a company can install a sensor on its transportation vehicles in order to provide clients with regular updates regarding the status of their shipments.

Implications

It is imperative for companies to remain updated on these advancements and reconfigure their value-generation procedures to center around the marketing of goods, which entails incorporating the customer's perspective within the company. The utilization of Internet of Things (IoT) technologies offers convenience and economic benefits to all involved parties. Our primary focus is to highlight the convenience for customers, as they are not required to invest excessive time in aimlessly navigating the store in quest of a specific, although relatively small, item. Furthermore, it is possible to create a specialized program that facilitates the acquisition of exclusive offers, enabling individuals to save on future purchases. The proliferation of technological advancements, such as the Internet of Things (IoT), has shown to be highly advantageous for businesses since it has the potential to greatly enhance the overall consumer experience. Managers possess the ability to promptly identify any deficiencies in operational duties and promptly rectify them in order to prevent any disruptions in customer service. Real-time monitoring is a crucial process that involves retrieving critical data, which plays a pivotal role in enhancing the quality of products or services. When prioritizing the enhancement of the overall customer experience, the consideration of adopting Internet of Things (IoT) technology into your organization arises. Organizations will want to enhance the consumer experience associated with their products or services. To achieve this, firms should contemplate the integration of

Internet of Things (IoT) technologies into their existing business operations. Contemporary customers are undergoing a transformation wherein they are increasingly acquainted with the concept of immediate accessibility. Consequently, they are developing expectations for their consumption and purchasing encounters to be characterized by expeditiousness, distinctiveness, and an emotional connection. Therefore, it is imperative for organizations to gain a comprehensive understanding of the fundamental shifts in consumer habits in order to effectively enhance and optimize customer experiences across both online and offline channels. In the preceding study, the emergence of a novel consumer was underscored, with particular emphasis placed on the evolution of the consumer's social standing, requirements, and position in the brand or company interaction.

CONCLUSION

In conclusion, the Internet of Things (IoT) is revolutionizing the dynamics between customers and companies, leading to a rapid transformation of our perceptions of the realm of possibilities. The Internet of Things (IoT) is increasingly being utilized in the field of customer experience management with the objective of enhancing customer pleasure, loyalty, and trust. Understanding the elements that define value for a client serves as the foundation for establishing an enduring rapport with the individual, leading to the development of a competitive edge for the organization. As the proliferation of connected devices and services continues to advance, facilitating the generation of data-driven insights for businesses, customers will not only experience the advantages but also assume a more significant role in shaping the evolution of organizations. The potential trajectory of the Internet of Things (IoT) remains uncertain, as it is intricately intertwined with forthcoming technological advancements. Nevertheless, it is evident that this phenomenon will have a substantial impact on several industries, companies, and brands in the foreseeable future. Simultaneously, it will enhance the client experience. While the definition of customer experience may encompass various crucial elements, its fundamental essence remains unchanged. The objective is to deliver optimal service to consumers and clients through both online and offline channels. The Internet of Things (IoT) presents a viable solution for enhancing customer experience. The Internet of Things (IoT) facilitates the augmentation and optimization of data transmission pertaining to customers' behaviors. The collection and analysis of data obtained from smart devices offer valuable insights into customers' purchasing and usage behaviors and patterns. The Internet of Things (IoT) facilitates the exploration of client behavior within its authentic context. The utilization of real-time data obtained from smart devices enables the ongoing monitoring of consumers' actions across different places, facilitating the identification of their interactions with items throughout their customer journey. The implementation of the Internet of Things (IoT) enables the provision of products with superior performance capabilities. The utilization of data collected through the Internet of Things (IoT) facilitates the monitoring of product performance and the implementation of updates that enhance customer satisfaction and foster continued engagement with a company. The Internet of Things (IoT) facilitates the establishment of robust client relationships through the provision of tailored services. Smart gadgets are utilized to provide customized services to customers with the intention of enhancing the relationship between the customer and a brand or corporation.

REFERENCES

Anand, A. (2023). How can you Improve Customer's Experience Using IoT? Available from: https://www.analyticssteps.com/blogs/how-can-you-improve-customers-experience-using-iot.

Belov, K. (2018). Customer Experience Management with IoT: 5 Components of the Successful Result. Available from: https://spur-i-t.com/blog/customer-experience-management-with-iot-5-components-of-the-successful-result/.

Britt, P. (2021). 4 Ways the Internet of Things Is Enhancing Customer Experience. Available from: https://www.cmswire.com/customer-experience/4-ways-the-internet-of-things-is-enhancing-customer-experience/.

Eguillor, M. (2018). IoT: A New Ally for Marketing. IoT: A New Ally for Marketing. IE Insights.

Gentile, C., Spiller, N., Noci, G. (2007). How to sustain the Customer Experience: An overview of experience components that co-create value with the customer. *Eur. Manage. J., 25*(5), 395-410. [http://dx.doi.org/10.1016/j.emj.2007.08.005]

Kocher, D. (2017). Customer Experience and the Internet of Things. Available from: https://www.ge.com/digital/blog.

Lemon, K.N., Verhoef, P.C. (2016). Understanding customer experience throughout the customer journey. *J. Mark., 80*(6), 69-96. [http://dx.doi.org/10.1509/jm.15.0420]

Lo, F.Y., Campos, N. (2018). Blending Internet-of-Things (IoT) solutions into relationship marketing strategies. *Technol. Forecast. Soc. Change, 137*, 10-18. [http://dx.doi.org/10.1016/j.techfore.2018.09.029]

Moradi, M. (2021). Importance of Internet of Things (IoT) in Marketing Research and Its Ethical and Data Privacy Challenges. *Business Ethics and Leadership, 5*(1), 22-30. [http://dx.doi.org/10.21272/bel.5(1).22-30.2021]

Ray, P.P. (2018). A survey on Internet of Things architectures. *Journal of King Saud University - Computer and Information Sciences, 30*(3), 291-319. [http://dx.doi.org/10.1016/j.jksuci.2016.10.003]

Reji, A. (2020). How to improve customer experience through IoT. Available from: https://lilacinfotech.com/blog/34/How-to-improve-customer-experience-through-IoT.

Ramirez, S. (2023). 4 Ways the Internet of Things is transforming customer experience. Available from: https://beyondthearc.com/blog/2016/customer-experience/4-ways-the-internet-of-things-is-transforming-customer-experience.

Sudolska, A. (2011). Zarządzanie doświadczeniami klientów jako kluczowy czynnik w procesie budowania ich lojalności. *Zeszyty Naukowe Uniwersytetu Szczecińskiego, 660*, 275-286.

Vermesan, O., Friess, P. (2014). Internet of Things applications: From research and innovation to market deployment, Gistrup, Denmark: River Publishers. Available from: https://www.riverpublishers.com/pdf/ebook/RP_E9788793102958.pdf.

CHAPTER 8

Internet of Things, Marketing, and Market Research

Benjamin NiiBoye Oda[1,*], **Bright Owusu Kwame**[1], **Banaba David Alaaba**[1], **Seidu Alhassan**[2] and **Mohammed Abdul-Basit Fuseini**[1]

[1] *Marketing Department, Tamale Technical University, Tamale, Ghana*

[2] *Secretaryship and Management Department, Tamale Technical University, Tamale, Ghana*

Abstract: Research is a systematic investigation of a specific subject, conducted with the aim of gathering empirical evidence and drawing logical inferences. Research is widely recognized as a key instrument due to its pivotal role as the initial phase in the marketing process. This chapter aims to investigate the utilization of Internet of Things (IoT) applications in the field of marketing and market research, with a specific focus on how firms employ IoT devices. No research is done today without technology tools such IoT and related technologies. Market research is employed as a means of gathering pertinent information regarding the market, encompassing customer demands, preferences, interests, market trends, and prevailing fashion, among other factors, *via* IoT. Marketing research is conducted with the objective of supplying managers with precise and reliable information to aid in making crucial marketing decisions. Therefore, market research is characterized by its specificity, as it provides insights and comprehension of a particular market that may not be applicable to other markets. On the other hand, marketing research is characterized by its generic nature, meaning that it has the potential to address a wide range of marketing issues.

Keywords: Internet of things, Market, Marketing, Research, Technology.

INTRODUCTION

The concept of the Internet of Things (IoT) has garnered significant attention in recent years, emerging as a prominent term in the technological landscape. However, it is only in recent times that the genuine transformative capabilities of this technology have started to become apparent. In its most basic form, the Internet of Things (IoT) refers to the notion of interconnectedness among many items seen in daily life, such as streetlights, industrial machinery, and wearable devices. These objects are equipped with sensors and are capable of wirelessly ex-

* **Corresponding author Benjamin NiiBoye Oda:** Marketing Department, Tamale Technical University, Tamale, Ghana; E-mail: bnboye@tatu.edu.gh

Mohammed Majeed, Jonas Yomboi, Sulemana Ibrahim & Esther Asiedu (Eds.)

changing pertinent data with one another. Given the proliferation of numerous applications now in operation, along with the continuous discovery of new ones, it is reasonable to anticipate that a significant portion of our daily existence will soon be influenced by Internet of Things (IoT) devices. In the contemporary era of consumer connectivity, there exists a convergence between the physical and digital realms, resulting in a symbiotic relationship where these two domains mutually engage. The integration of big data, analytics, and mobile technologies facilitates the seamless sharing and collection of data among various objects and devices within a linked network, with minimal reliance on human interaction. According to Chhatwal (2023), the utilization of the Internet of Things (IoT) offers several advantages, including cost reduction, enhanced production and efficiency, and heightened convenience. In essence, the Internet of Things (IoT) offers considerable advantages to companies and market researchers by furnishing them with a vast array of consumer behavior data that can be effectively leveraged to enhance their financial performance. Smartphone applications provide consumers with the opportunity to engage in product experimentation within the realm of beauty prior to committing to a purchase. Market analysts must prioritize industries that are relevant to IoT adoption when attempting to identify future trends. This chapter aims to investigate the utilization of Internet of Things (IoT) applications in the field of marketing and market research, with a specific focus on how firms employ IoT devices.

LITERATURE REVIEW

Internet of Things

According to Javaid and Khan (2021), the Internet of Things (IoT) facilitates the transmission and reception of both information and physical items *via* the Internet. Smart hospital technologies and concepts are regulated by both wireless and fixed internet connectivity. The use of the Internet of Things (IoT) in the medical area relies heavily on a range of medical devices, diagnostics, sensors, advanced imaging technologies, and artificial intelligence. In order to fulfill the necessary objective, intelligent gadgets have the capability to exchange and record data within the context of everyday activities. This application is being implemented in various domains, including residential environments, smart urban areas, leisure platforms, automotive systems, and interconnected healthcare services.

Marketing and Market Research

Research is commonly characterized as a dynamic, conscientious, and methodical endeavor of investigation with the objective of uncovering, interpreting, and refining factual information. These two names have a semblance of synonymity, even with a distinction of merely three letters; nonetheless, they are not truly synonymous. It is important to differentiate between market research and marketing research. Market research often includes studies and investigations pertaining to the market, while marketing research involves actions focused on marketing-related research.

Market Research

Market research is conducted to determine the viability of a novel service or product through the implementation of customer surveys and direct study. Market research allows a company to discern its target market and get feedback and various forms of customer input regarding their level of interest in a certain product or service (Vexco, 2023). Market research is a systematic investigation that analyzes the market for a specific commodity or service in order to ascertain the potential response of the target audience. The process may entail gathering data for the purpose of market segmentation and product differentiation, enabling the customization of advertising strategies, or the identification of traits that are perceived as significant by the consumer. In order to complete the market research process, a corporation is required to undertake a number of duties. Data collection is crucial and should be tailored to the specific market sector being analyzed (Vexco, 2023). The analysis and interpretation of the collected data are necessary for the company to assess the existence of patterns or significant data points that can inform the decision-making process. Market research plays a crucial role in facilitating firms' comprehension of the demand and viability of their products, as well as their potential performance in real-world settings (Vexco, 2023). Market research is conducted by utilizing primary or secondary data sources which offer unique perspectives on a company's product. Market research plays a crucial role in the research and development (R&D) phase of a firm, contributing significantly to its achievements and expansion. The principal objective of engaging in market research is to get insights into the market pertaining to a specific product or service, with the aim of determining the anticipated response of the target audience towards that product or service. The data acquired *via* the implementation of market research can be utilized to customize marketing and advertising strategies or ascertain the preferences and needs of consumers. Market research explores several aspects of the target market, including their requirements, desires, spending patterns, and traits. Additionally, it can draw comparisons with both competitors and prevailing industry benchmarks. Market research serves as the initial step for businesses to evaluate the feasibility of introducing new goods or services to their intended market. During the course of this process, it frequently uncovers previously unidentified target markets and discerns client desires and requirements.

Marketing Research

The field of marketing research involves the systematic gathering, analysis, and interpretation of data in order to gain insights into consumer behavior. Marketing research is a methodical process that involves the systematic collection, documentation, and analysis of both qualitative and quantitative data pertaining to the marketing of goods and services. Marketing research is a methodical and unbiased examination of issues related to the marketing of products and services. This concept can be used in various domains within the field of marketing. Research is the sole instrument that a company possesses to maintain communication with its external operating environment. Marketing research encompasses a wider scope than market research since it pertains to the comprehensive examination of marketing's four fundamental elements, sometimes referred to as the four Ps: product, price, place, and promotion. Marketing research is a methodical process that involves the collection, documentation, and examination of both qualitative and quantitative data pertaining to matters concerning the promotion and sale of products and services. The objective of marketing research is to detect and evaluate the effects of modifying components of the marketing mix on customer behavior. The word "marketing research" is sometimes used interchangeably with "market research", while some experts prefer to differentiate between the two. They argue that market research focuses solely on marketplaces, whereas marketing research explicitly examines marketing processes. The objective of this study is to investigate and evaluate the impact of modifying marketing mix components on consumer behavior. This encompasses the process of determining the necessary data for addressing these issues, formulating the approach for acquiring information, and overseeing and executing the data collection procedure (Vexco, 2023). Upon thorough examination of the obtained data, the resulting conclusions, findings, and implications are communicated to individuals with the necessary power and jurisdiction to take appropriate actions based on the information presented. The primary objective of marketing research (MR) is to provide management with pertinent, precise, reliable, valid, and current knowledge (Vexco, 2023). The delivery of high-quality information in marketing research is imperative due to the intensely competitive nature of the marketing environment and the escalating costs associated with poor decision-making. Sound judgments are not solely based on instinctual feelings, intuition, or even strict logical reasoning.

Impact of IoT on Marketing Research

The advent of technology has revolutionized the methods employed by organizations in conducting market research. Conventional research techniques, such as surveys and focus groups, have been augmented with advanced tools that facilitate the collection and processing of data in real time. Social media listening solutions provide the real-time monitoring of consumer sentiments towards a company's brand, competitors, and the industry. Machine learning algorithms possess the capability to evaluate extensive datasets, hence facilitating the extraction of valuable information pertaining to consumer behavior and the identification of previously overlooked trends. Augmented reality (AR) and artificial intelligence (AI) are being employed to replicate shopping experiences and collect feedback from consumers within a controlled setting. Market researchers possess a natural inclination to proactively anticipate future trends while also devoting adequate attention to the current and historical aspects of their work. The "Internet of everything" represents the anticipated progression of the Internet of Things (IoT), wherein the emphasis extends beyond the interconnectedness of equipment involved in data transmission to encompass the manner in which data is exchanged. The advent of big data analytics has significantly enhanced the potential value of interconnected devices and services, ushering in a new era. Researchers are increasingly acquiring the capacity to meticulously evaluate datasets and derive practical insights and informative value from seemingly ordinary, routine phenomena. The prominence of qualitative research in the field of the Internet of Things (IoT) is expected to increase. Moving forward, given that researchers are now in the exploratory stage of the Internet of Things (IoT) phenomenon, it is anticipated that qualitative investigations will yield more definitive outcomes. The rationale for avoiding a quantitative survey lies in the inherent limitations associated with relying predominantly on conjecture, as well as the potential for inadequate comprehension of the survey questions due to the confusing nature of the subject matter by a significant portion of respondents. Hence, conducting a qualitative inquiry that explores individuals' actions pertaining to the Internet of Things (IoT), the significance of IoT in their endeavors, and the unanticipated challenges encountered has the potential to provide novel insights for your research (Roznovsky, 2023).

Pursuing Consumer Behavior

The study of consumer behavior involves the systematic observation and analysis of individuals' actions, decisions, and preferences in relation to the acquisition, usage, and disposal of goods and services. The Internet of Things (IoT) refers to a network of interconnected gadgets that are capable of intelligent communication and operation *via* the Internet. The availability of data has expanded beyond smartphones and computers to include a wide range of devices, such as smart appliances, wearable technologies, cars, and networked gadgets (Chhatwal, 2023). In an era characterized by extensive connectivity and a predominant reliance on digital platforms, data offers a substantial amount of insight into consumer routines and behaviors. The utilization of interconnected sensors in the implementation of automated scheduling and monitoring facilitates enhanced resource efficiency, including more effective power management and water consumption. For instance, the implementation of basic motion detectors has the potential to yield substantial cost savings in terms of electricity and water use. Consequently, this can enhance the productivity and environmental sustainability of organizations, regardless of their scale. The connectivity of smart devices provides a notable advantage in the form of automated control across several operational domains, such as inventory management, shipping tracking, and fuel and spare parts management, to name a few. One illustrative method entails the utilization of RFID tags in conjunction with a network of sensors to monitor and ascertain the whereabouts of equipment and merchandise. According to Roznovsky (2023), the presence of smart devices in residential settings, particularly voice assistants and other appliances capable of direct and regular communication with end-users, offers a significant and indispensable resource for doing business analysis. The Internet of Things (IoT) facilitates organizations by collecting substantial amounts of user-specific data, which may be utilized for the purpose of formulating corporate strategies, implementing targeted advertising campaigns, refining pricing policies, and conducting various marketing and management endeavors. The aforementioned aggregation of user-specific data obtained through the utilization of smart devices also facilitates organizations in gaining a deeper comprehension of client expectations and behavior. The Internet of Things (IoT) enhances customer service by enabling post-sales follow-ups, including automated tracking and reminders for consumers regarding necessary maintenance of acquired equipment once its predetermined duration of use has elapsed, as well as the expiration of warranty periods (Roznovsky, 2023). As a result of heightened efficiency, the utilization of IoT solutions by a corporation enables the provision of a broader array of services or products or the enhancement of their quality vis-à-vis competitors while maintaining price parity. In lieu of the aforementioned, a corporation of this nature may undertake more arduous endeavors in relation to production complexity, duration, or volume. On the whole, the use of intelligent solutions enhances the competitiveness and desirability of a firm as a prospective business collaborator (Vexco, 2023). The corporate landscape is undergoing rapid transformation, rendering traditional methods of consumer connection outdated. In order to effectively engage with technologically savvy consumers, it is imperative for companies to embrace digital data collecting and analysis. The Internet of Things (IoT) is a highly important and precise instrument for the monitoring of a product's functioning, as well as the analysis of user behavior, preferences, and attitudes towards said product. The Internet of Things (IoT) has the potential to provide valuable insights to brands regarding areas for improvement in their products and messaging (Chhatwal, 2023).

Experimentation

The primary aim of integrating the Internet of Things (IoT) into laboratory settings is to enhance the efficiency and efficacy of experimental procedures and data collection for research purposes. The integration of Internet of Things (IoT) enabled devices will enhance the connectivity of many laboratory components, ranging from scales to centrifuges. According to Chubb (2020), the utilization of this technology enables the direct transmission of machine output into a digital format, resulting in significant time and effort savings for scientists while also eliminating the potential for human error. In an Internet of Things (IoT)-enabled laboratory, all devices are interconnected with either a cloud or local server. This connectivity allows researchers to remotely operate the equipment and access them from any location with an internet connection. By establishing a network of interconnected devices and sensors that are integrated into a central system, researchers can enhance the efficiency of their experiments by minimizing obstacles and reducing error-related problems. The Internet of Things (IoT) has a diverse range of manifestations within laboratory settings, with automation being the prevailing type. According to Chubb (2020), certain vendors suggest that the optimal approach would involve the automation of all laboratory equipment, including material containers. Nevertheless, this approach can frequently incur significant costs, rendering it accessible solely to prosperous industry research facilities. An additional approach to incorporating the Internet of Things (IoT) into laboratory settings involves the utilization of a laboratory execution system. This system facilitates the connection between pre-existing laboratory equipment and the internet, enabling not only the control and monitoring of these devices but also the management of automated devices such as collaborative robots (co-bots) and pipetting robots.

Projecting Consumer Behavior

Projecting consumer behavior is analyzed in order to determine the optimal timing for sales.

The Internet of Things (IoT) facilitates the ability of brands to discern consumer needs, hence providing advantages to both brands and researchers (Chhatwal, 2023). This can be utilized as a means of promoting establishments that provide the service. Consequently, it enhances the overall sales performance.

Providing Customized Experiences

According to Chhatwal (2023), the incorporation of analysis of data into brand operations enables the provision of personalized experiences and facilitates the acquisition of insights into consumer behavior. The past two decades have witnessed significant transformations in technology and consumer behavior. The Internet of Things (IoT) offers a valuable source of data for market researchers, facilitating a deeper understanding of customer behavior and preferences. This enhanced understanding enables market researchers to generate reports and analyses for brands that are characterized by accuracy, impartiality, and a focus on actionable insights, devoid of any potential human errors (Roznovsky, 2023).

Interconnected and Secure Infrastructure

The integration of university infrastructure with the gadgets utilized by researchers, students, and professors facilitates enhanced planning and utilization of instructional spaces by university employees. Students have the opportunity to ascertain beforehand the availability of a study pod, as well as the feasibility of collaborating with their peers remotely. According to Roznovsky (2023), researchers have the ability to ascertain the real-time availability of their laboratory or reserve an alternative laboratory space.

The utilization of Internet of Things (IoT) technologies has the potential to enhance researchers' networks within related fields, foster interdisciplinary connections among traditionally isolated disciplines, and facilitate the discovery of novel insights inside academic articles. Additionally, it has the capability to identify issues inside research endeavors, highlighting the potential for collaborative efforts to enhance outcomes for all involved parties. Artificial intelligence (AI) possesses the capability to consolidate, curate, and facilitate the analytical processes of students and researchers, enabling them to concentrate on their specific requirements.

The Cloud and IoT go Hand in Hand

Internet of Things (IoT) sensors possess inherent internet connectivity, facilitating the exchange of data through cloud-based platforms. The Internet of Things (IoT) has significant ramifications in the domains of cloud computing, streaming analytics, big data, and data visualization (Roznovsky, 2023). Market researchers have the opportunity to access vast quantities of data for examination, enabling them to gather, process, and analyze this data effectively. Consequently, cloud companies like Microsoft Azure and Amazon Web Services can get significant advantages from this situation.

Old School Industries are the Pioneers of Adopting New Technologies

Market researchers typically regard the technology industry as the primary early adopters of novel technical advancements and direct their attention and study accordingly. However, in the realm of market research, it is the traditional industries such as manufacturing, government, oil and gas, among others, that are at the forefront of driving the Internet of Things (IoT) revolution. The Internet of Things (IoT) has gained significant traction in various industries. It has been utilized for diverse purposes, such as detecting pressure drops in oil pipelines and monitoring traffic and parking within urban areas. Notably, the adoption of IoT has been particularly noteworthy in industries that typically exhibit a conservative approach towards technology implementation, which otherwise progresses at a slower pace.

Hardware and Software

The Internet of Things (IoT) is a network of interconnected physical devices and vehicles. The relationship between hardware and software is a fundamental aspect of computer systems. The primary focus of interest and research lies in the hardware sensors and their diverse variations. However, market researchers must also direct their attention toward the fundamental software infrastructure responsible for efficiently transmitting substantial volumes of data from one location to another, frequently in real time. Researchers can potentially discover valuable information that could otherwise be overlooked by directing their attention toward the programming that enables devices to function.

Security

The fundamental emphasis lies on the security of research issues. The primary objective of the Internet of Things (IoT) is to facilitate the seamless exchange and distribution of data. Consequently, numerous prominent firms in this industry, including Microsoft and Cisco, will undertake the development of safe IoT devices and allocate substantial financial resources toward enhancing the security of the Internet of Things. This concerted effort aims to establish a fair playing field for a diverse range of devices inside the realm of IoT. Simultaneously, this domain will also allure numerous companies that may lack substantial financial resources for development, thereby rendering the security of the gadget uncertain. The cost of constructing a safe entity is invariably higher, thus necessitating a heightened emphasis on the security aspect of numerous research endeavors. To what extent does the general population demonstrate concern for security in the Internet of Things (IoT)? To what extent does security influence individuals' purchasing behavior? These types of inquiries can assist market researchers in inferring forthcoming patterns.

Implications

Management should collaborate with security program staff to determine the nature and severity of both internal and external hazards to the protection of protected gadgets and networking that can lead to unlawful entry to or unapproved alteration of a covered device or network and to evaluate the effectiveness of existing controls to mitigate those threats. When trying to determine what kinds of networked devices might be involved in an IoT ecosystem, it can be useful to draw a diagram of the system. Researchers, in coordination with leadership, should establish a regular timetable for conducting confidential and safe risk evaluations as well as a process for conducting and reviewing this research in order to enact any necessary modifications.

CONCLUSION

The laboratory setting is ideal for introducing IoT because of its specific characteristics. Increased productivity from the Internet of Things (IoT)-enabled devices might significantly boost discovery yield if these factors were prioritized. Investigators are searching for ways to ensure their research is readily available in compliance without having to purchase expensive new laboratory equipment. This is because the scientific community adheres to a strict set of measures and regulations, such as FAIR (ensuring research is findable, accessible, interoperable, and replicable). In contrast to market research, marketing research encompasses a broader set of activities. In fact, studies on the market are a subset of marketing studies. Focus groups, surveys (telephone or face-to-face), screenings, and surveys are all used in both quantitative and qualitative studies. In addition, the studies are of great assistance to both new and established businesses in making important choices about their product or service offerings, locations for operations, marketing strategies, and other operational aspects. Potentially fruitful developments lie ahead for market research in the digital age. Businesses' data collection and analysis processes are evolving as a result of new technologies, the proliferation of connected devices, and the demand for more nuanced, individualized understandings. The future of market research is bright for companies that adapt to new tools and modify their strategies based on the demographics of their customers. Businesses may thrive and succeed when they have access to the data and insights made possible by the Internet of Things (IoT).

REFERENCES

Chhatwal, G. (2023). The Importance of the Internet of Things (IoT) for Brands and Market Research. Available from: https://kadence.com/the-importance-of-iot-for-brands-and-market-research/#:~:text=IoT %20provides%20data%20that%20can,information%20free%20from%20human%20error.

Chubb, P. (March 26, 2020). Smart Labs: How IoT is Revolutionizing Research and Development. Available from: https://www.iotforall.com/iot-research-development#:~:text=By%20implementing%20IoT%20into

%20the,and%20research%20is%20more%20accessible.

Javaid, M., Khan, I.H. (2021). Internet of Things (IoT) enabled healthcare helps to take the challenges of COVID-19 Pandemic. *J. Oral Biol. Craniofac. Res., 11*(2), 209-214.
[http://dx.doi.org/10.1016/j.jobcr.2021.01.015] [PMID: 33665069]

Roznovsky, A. (2023). 9 Prominent Benefits of IoT for Business. Available from: https://light-it.net/blog/-prominent-benefits-of-iot-for-business/.

Vexco, (2023). Market Research vs. Marketing Research: Similarities & Differences. Available from: https://www.voxco.com/blog/market-research-vs-marketing-research/.

CHAPTER 9

Smart Manufacturing for Fashion Firms

Abas Sherifatu[1,*], **Joana Akweley Zanu**[1], **Musah Bukari**[1] and **Eunice Acheampomaa Ameyaw**[1]

[1] *Department of Graphic Communication Design Technology, Tamale Technical University, Tamale, Ghana*

Abstract: Industries in many parts of the world today have evolved as a result of rapid advancement in information and manufacturing technologies. In Ghana, the product manufacturing subsector, of which the fashion industry is a part, has also continued to evolve just as the technological advancement progresses. As a result, companies (fashion houses) are consistently looking for innovative ways to adapt to the ever-growing demands of consumer's trendy wear. In view of the fact that the world is experiencing low growth in the global economy, the fashion industry, realizing this, has adopted smart manufacturing to enable it to maintain its relevance in the global economy. Thus, smartening up factories is crucial in this era of industrial revolutions. The traditional methods of operation by the fashion industry continue to fade as e-commerce booms. There is a need for the fashion industry to evolve by adopting smart manufacturing, which may help the textile and garment industries become more environmentally responsible and efficient, as well as boost business output and efficiency by equipping "smart factories" with automated processes and technological advancements. The purpose of this chapter is to review the literature on key areas of smart manufacturing for fashion firms. It has been revealed in the chapter that the projected advantages of the fourth industrial revolution are being fulfilled by smart manufacturing projects. By integrating digital technologies with traditional automated manufacturing processes, the manufacturing industry is projected to see a new growth trajectory. More so, the smart factory can actively participate in the transition of industries by utilizing the internet, data analytics, and sensors. This will eventually lead to technological advancement at all stages of the manufacturing process. However, not every firm will be able to balance the benefits of upgrading technology, installing security systems, and retraining workers against the associated costs. Making a factory smart requires input from many departments within a firm, but ultimately, the decision must be taken on an accurate assessment of its financial viability for the facility or business model in question.

Keywords: Augmented reality, Artificial intelligence, Fashion firms, IoT, Virtual reality, Smart manufacturing.

* **Corresponding author Abas Sherifatu:** Department of Graphic Communication Design Technology, Tamale Technical University, Tamale, Ghana; E-mail: asheriatu@tatu.edu.gh

INTRODUCTION

Companies are looking for innovative ways to adapt to the ever-evolving demands of consumers as a result of globalization and the rapid advancement of computer technology (Ge, Liu & Ma, 2018). Smartening up factories is crucial in the Fifth Industrial Revolution. This is due to the fact that we have entered a period of low growth in the global economy. The fashion industry has realized that adopting smart manufacturing (Internet of Things (IoT), virtual reality (VR), augmented reality (AR), artificial intelligence (AI), *etc.*) is crucial to its continued success (Lee, Ju & Lee, 2021). The term "Industry 5.0" describes an environment where humans and intelligent machines operate together. With the help of cutting-edge tools like the Internet of Things (IoT) and big data, robots can improve human productivity. Technology and efficiency are the cornerstones of Industry 4.0, and they bring a human dimension. All sectors will be affected by the emerging global ecosystem that is Industry 5.0. Humans and machines may finally find common ground thanks to Industry 5.0 (Martins, 2022). The ultimate objective is to combine the unmatched creative problem-solving abilities of humans with the unmatched cognitive perfection of robots in order to design and implement effective processes. With the help of IoT and AI, the fashion industry has completely revamped its supply chain, allowing for instantaneous reactions and widespread customization. Traditional offline market structures have been disrupted by the advent of e-commerce, which reduces the time and distance between sellers and customers. As e-commerce continues to boom, even more so during the epidemic, it is altering the fashion industry's traditional methods of operation (Lee *et al.*, 2021). As an added bonus, smart manufacturing may help the textile and garment industries become more environmentally responsible and efficient. In addition, businesses have attempted to boost output and efficiency by equipping "smart factories" with automated processes and technological advancements (Industrynews, 2018). Keeping up with the times and remaining competitive in today's industry require a constant focus on digital innovation. The garment industry has recently begun digitizing its operations to get vital data and develop insights. The value of data has expanded beyond process monitoring to include a better grasp of what is most important to customers and how to best meet their demands (Apparel Resources, 2018). Technology from the areas of production, information, and communication is part of a "smart factory", with the latter two having the potential to be integrated throughout the entire supply chain.

According to Hsieh (2021), global retail sales fell in 2020 for the first time since the 1960s. Likewise, as a result of the epidemic, technology-based manufacturing and online retail sales increased dramatically. In reality, there was a 36.6% rise in global traffic to e-commerce sites between January 2020 and June 2020. There would be more than $4 trillion in global e-commerce sales by the end of 2020, or

18% of all retail sales (Hsieh, 2021). By 2025, it is expected that online shopping will make up at least 25% of all retail sales. There is no denying that this is an issue that demands attention from the business world, specifically in the digital sphere. When it comes to retail e-commerce sales in the United States, the clothing and accessories industry is currently in second place, with a share of 20.7%. The global value of all fashion items sold online is projected to hit $953 billion by 2024, growing at a CAGR of 12.7%. The purpose of this chapter is to review the literature on key areas of smart manufacturing for fashion firms.

LITERATURE

Smart Manufacturing

In order to establish a more advantageous system for businesses that focus on manufacturing and supply chain management, the term "smart factory" refers to a factory in which traditional production processes and operations are integrated with digital technology, smart computing, and big data (Sarkar, 2020). Flexibility in production, mass customization, higher quality, and higher productivity are the goals of smart manufacturing, also known as Industry 4.0. (Zhong *et al.*, 2017). Industry 5.0, the next stage of the Industrial Revolution, places a premium on actual statistics, sensor technology, networking, automation, and algorithms; a smart factory is one manifestation of this trend. Industry 5.0 manufacturing will involve the use of machine learning, robotics, AI, the IoT, data analytics, and augmented/virtual reality (Sarkar, 2020). Establishing a digitally-enabled "smart factory" is one of several viable options for improving efficiency and productivity in the workplace. By implementing a smart factory, a company can prevent operational downtime and other productivity difficulties because of the smart factory's capacity to adapt and learn from data in real time (Jagdish, 2018). According to Jagdish (2018), "only the appropriate kind of data used in the right setting with the right people behind it assists in creating the big improvements.'

A smart factory is a manufacturing facility that is capable of autonomously connecting, collecting, and analyzing data through the use of Internet of Things (IoT) devices for communication (Kim & Moon, 2020). Building a fashion system on the backs of product quantities that are more in sync with market demand, more in line with consumers' expectations, highly customizable, and transparent throughout their whole lifecycle is possible with the help of smart factory and automation technologies (Bertola &Teunissen, 2018). The cutting, sewing, and inventory divisions in the savvy fashion sectors have improved the quality of the fabric used in making blazers and jackets that are made to order. Fabric, raw materials, order status, and blazer pressing are all monitored *via* the barcode system. Its complex manufacturing system may be monitored in a more coordinated fashion with the use of a barcode system (Zhong *et al.*, 2017). Gas chutes for fixing broken trimmings and automated fabric inspection machines have both been implemented to improve working conditions. Audio activity is sampled virtually, and shipments and stock levels are tracked using digital technology (Zhong *et al.*, 2017).

Type of Technologies Used in Smart Manufacturing

A smart factory is a fully automated and digitalized manufacturing facility that collects and shares data in real time from its various linked devices, machines, and production systems. The collected information is then used to solve problems and enhance operations. Artificial intelligence (AI), big data analytics, cloud computing, and the industrial Internet of Things (IoT) are just a few of the technologies that enable the smart manufacturing techniques utilized by a smart factory (BlackSmith International, 2021).

Connectivity

Facilitating communication amongst staff members also aids in ensuring a smooth operation. It has never been simpler to reach out to others because of the plethora of available apps, such as chatbots. The manufacturing, inspection, and industrial designers can respond to the problem in real-time. Data and images can be shared in real time, providing immediate feedback and aiding in the making of decisions (BlackSmith International, 2021). This can be used to intervene in a process before it has a chance to affect the final result by halting, changing, altering, or addressing it.

RFID

In the last few decades, RFID technology has been used in the manufacturing process to facilitate a more streamlined and methodical flow of materials. The possibility of developing a flawless production system is raised by this method. The signal is transmitted to the machines *via* microchips placed in the product. Potentially, the machine's functioning can be started and stopped with information transmitted through RFID tags.

Robotics

With the use of robotic procedure automation, they are able to get rid of the things that do not bring value and cut down on the number of times people have to step in. In the cutting stage of garment production, they have implemented AI to estimate fabric consumption and enhance quality control; they have also implemented AI to generate advisory warning signals at key points in the process

(BlackSmith International, 2021). Despite their extensive use in manufacturing processes, robots still do not have any truly intelligent traits. In the past, robots needed a human operator in order to perform any task (Görçün, 2018). Communication between robots and materials, whether they are raw, semi-finished, or finished goods, is possible. They can also cause changes in the way logistics are handled. In the future, each step in the value chain will act as a trigger for the next, and the entire process will be carried out without any human interaction (Görçün, 2018).

Virtual Reality and Augmented Reality

Virtual reality is a more immersive virtual environment that requires special glasses, whereas augmented reality is a digital technology that involves digital information being superimposed over reality and seen *via* a smartphone. Both of these innovations can facilitate the management of products, manufacturing duties, and equipment maintenance and repair in a smart industrial setting (BlackSmith International, 2021).

Digital Twins

A digital twin is a virtual representation of a real-world system or object that can be used to model its behavior. Because of this, efficiency can be increased, and control and operations planning can be aided.

Internet of Things

The term "Internet of Things" (IoTs) refers to the interconnection and exchange of data between physical objects that have acquired digital identities and capabilities thanks to technological developments (BlackSmith International, 2021). The term "Internet of Things" (IoT) refers to a network of interconnected physical devices, equipment, and/or processes that exchange data and instructions over the Internet and with one another and with humans. As a result of these interconnections, the formerly dumb physical systems are now capable of doing several industrial processes on their own. In the Internet of Things (IoT), physical things are easily incorporated into the data network, where they can take part in operational procedures (Görçün, 2018). Industrial Internet of Things (IoT) devices are cloud-connected sensors and physical items that collect data from industrial facilities and either transport it to servers or process it immediately through edge computing. Some Internet of Things devices are set up to work with sensors already installed in buildings, while others collect information from remote sensors and forward it on. The high cost of commercial IoT equipment makes its adoption by SMEs difficult (Rauch, 2019). When everything is connected to the internet, it opens the door to possibilities for integration across all business operations, including production and consumption along value chains. Additionally, businesses may learn what consumers want and need. When this technology is put to good use, it is simple to learn about customers' wants and needs.

Sensors

At several points in the production process, data is collected from sensors on equipment and machines (BlackSmith International, 2021). Sensors can check the temperature or other conditions and either fix themselves or notify humans if something goes wrong. These sensors, when connected to a network, can provide unified machine-wide monitoring.

Computer-Assisted Design (CAD) System

Digital 2D and 3D sketching are possible using CAD software. For some time now, digital printing technology, such as 3D printers, has been a game-changer in the fashion industry. By accommodating consumers' varying tastes in terms of aesthetics (such as color scheme and pattern preference), this technology has enhanced the quality of product design. 3D printing is an expensive procedure that is more in line with the budgets of corporate fashion companies than independent labels. Nevertheless, it is a useful tool for reducing waste and avoiding mistakes during the design phase. Successful platforms like AutoDesk or Eva Engines, the latter of which converts sketches into 2D product pictures for developers, demonstrate the usefulness of this database connection across the production chain.

Benefits of SM

The garment sector can now respond to customers' wants and needs in real time thanks to the advancements made possible by Industry 4.0 and 5.0 technology (BlackSmith International, 2021). Millennials and other younger consumers prefer customized goods over those that are mass-produced yet fail to reflect their unique tastes (Twi Global, 2022). With the help of Industry 5.0, clothing manufacturers can respond rapidly to changing consumer tastes, even when manufacturing in bulk (Geek, 2020). By diminishing the need for human intervention, increasing the speed with which products may be brought to market, cutting down on raw wastage of materials, and decreasing manufacturing costs, SM improves efficiency all around.

Connected machinery and tools in "smart" factories facilitate data-driven information processing, which in turn increases output and cuts costs. The manufacturing sector can benefit from decreased costs, fewer downtimes, and less waste if agile, iterative production processes are implemented (Twi Global, 2022). Before the advent of Industry 4.0, it took two years or more for a garment to go from a Paris runway display to a factory production line. Many of these fads in apparel do not do well in sales when they are finally made; therefore, hundreds of pounds of garbage is produced (BlackSmith International, 2021). The garment business is the second-largest polluter in the world, after the oil industry, according to the Fashion Industry Waste Statistics. Today, businesses may respond to customers' wants and demands in terms of apparel with minimal waste, thanks to real-time input (Geek, 2020). Satisfaction soars among buyers when a clothing retailer meets their demands for speedy shipping, reasonable prices, and high-quality goods (BlackSmith International, 2021). When customers are happy, they are also more inclined to continue buying from you. By locating idle or misplaced production capacities and then eliminating or minimizing them, efficiency and output can be increased with minimal outlay of new resources (Twi Global, 2022). When a factory is digitized, real-time data is used to evaluate and improve planning, quality control, product development, and logistics.

Businesses in the fashion industry can boost customer loyalty, retail contracts, and market share by tailoring their products to meet the needs of specific demographics of consumers. As a result of automation made possible by Industry 5.0, clothing manufacturers can now see their products through the entire process, from design to production (Geek, 2020). This means that a clothing brand can make a regular line for widespread distribution alongside more limited edition capsule and seasonal lines without compromising on quality. Between 5% and 30% of annual revenue can be lost due to subpar quality. Industry 4.0 has the potential to make low-quality clothing obsolete. Access to real-time quality data and information sharing that monitors processes, machines, and people is now possible in smart factories (Geek, 2020). This allows the apparel industry to speed up the rate of improvement while simultaneously cutting the price of quality. Integrating machine learning into the procedure also has long-term advantages. Production line shutdowns can be avoided by the use of data collection and analysis in the form of preventative and predictive maintenance (Twi Global, 2022).

The Future of Smart Manufacturing

Some textile mills of the future will undergo a metamorphosis into "smart factories". By automating tasks like production planning, order fulfillment, employee training, and data collection and analysis in real-time, they will have greater influence over all aspects of their organization. However, traditional garment manufacturing will still be around. Many garment companies are now investing in cloud-based, SAAS-based technologies to prepare for the forthcoming digital revolution. The shifts in perspective make it feasible to achieve all of these goals. The shifts will be brought about through reasonable investment and improved solutions. The fashion industry relies heavily on originality; thus, it is crucial that designers understand and meet the needs of their customers. One commodity that consistently sees great demand is tailor-made apparel. Computer-aided manufacturing systems have made it possible for clothing manufacturers to experiment with mass customization methods.

CONCLUSION

Many of the projected advantages of the fourth industrial revolution are being fulfilled by SM projects. By fusing digital technologies with traditional automated manufacturing processes, the manufacturing industry is anticipated to see a new growth trajectory. Now is the time for businesses to act and adopt SM if they want to properly develop resilience. Utilizing a variety of technologies, smart factories can develop connected manufacturing that can gather and analyze process data and result in enhancements to productivity, safety, and other factors. Improvements in procedures, inspection and maintenance, logistics, timeliness, and even employee utilization can all be a part of this optimization. A smart factory can actively participate in the transition to Industry 4.0 by utilizing the Internet of Things, data analytics, and sensors. This will result in improvements felt throughout the entire manufacturing process. However, not every firm will be able to balance the benefits of upgrading technology, installing security systems, and retraining workers against the associated costs. Making a factory smart requires input from many departments within a firm, but ultimately, the decision must be founded on an accurate assessment of its financial viability for the facility or business model in question.

REFERENCES

Apparel Resources (2018). Framework for evolving from Traditional to Smart Factory. Available from: https://apparelresources.com/technology-news/manufacturing-tech/framework-evolving-traditional--mart-factory/.

Bertola, P., & Teunissen, J. (2018). Fashion 4.0. Innovating fashion industry through digital transformation. *Research journal of textile and apparel*, *22*(4), 352-369.

BlackSmith International (2021). Smart Factories: The Future of Apparel Manufacturing. Available from: https://blacksmithint.com/smart-factories-the-future-of-apparel-manufacturing/.

Geek (2020). 3 Key Elements of Smart Factory. Available from: https://blog.geekplus.com/company/news-center/3-key-elements-of-smart-factory.

Hsieh, P. (2021). Impact of e-commerce, smart manufacturing on fashion industry. 2021 World digital textile forum: Digitalization in fashion. Available from: https://www.digitimes.com/news/a20211203PR200.html&chid=9.

Industrynews (2018). Why Smart Factory is Important in the 4th Industrial Revolution Era. 2018.02.18. Available from: http://industrynews.co.kr/ news/articleView.html?idxno=21427.

Jagdish R. (2018). Framework for evolving from Traditional to Smart Factory.

Kim, J.C., Moon, I.Y. (2020). A study on smart factory construction method for efficient production management in sewing industry. *J. Inf. Commun. Converg. Eng., 18*, 61-68.

Lee, S., Rho, S.H., Lee, S., Lee, J., Lee, S.W., Lim, D., Jeong, W. (2021). Implementation of an automated manufacturing process for smart clothing: The case study of a smart sports bra. *Processes (Basel), 9*(2), 289. [http://dx.doi.org/10.3390/pr9020289]

Lee, S.E., Ju, N., Lee, K.H. (2021). Visioning the future of smart fashion factories based on media big data analysis. *Appl. Sci. (Basel), 11*(16), 7549. [http://dx.doi.org/10.3390/app11167549]

Martins A. (2022). Industry 5.0: How the Mass Customization Era Can Be the Solution to Overproduction. Platform. Available from: https://www.platforme.com/blog/industry-5-0-how-the-mass-customizat-on-era-can-be-the-solution-for-overproduction.

Sarkar P. (2020). The Smart Garment Factory - Concepts, Technology and Future (with Two Cases). Available from: https://www.onlineclothingstudy.com/2020/08/the-smart-garment-factory-concepts.html.

Twi Global (2022). What is a smart factory? (A complete guide). Available from: https://www.twi-global.com/technical-knowledge/faqs/what-is-a-smart-factory.

Zhong, R.Y., Xu, X., Klotz, E., Newman, S.T. (2017). Intelligent manufacturing in the context of industry 4.0: A review. *Engineering (Beijing), 3*(5), 616-630. [http://dx.doi.org/10.1016/J.ENG.2017.05.015]

SUBJECT INDEX

A

Accelerated legal claims 113
Adopting new technologies 126
Advertising campaigns 40, 123
AI-powered personalization engines 57
Amazon web services 125
Antimicrobial coatings 27
Appliances 7, 24, 69, 84, 104, 123
  domestic 84
  household 104
  voice-enabled kitchen 24
Applications 7, 9, 15, 52, 61, 65, 94, 96, 97, 99, 119
  fertilizer 9
  implementing 99
  industrial 52
  mobile 15, 61, 96
  of internet of things 65, 94
  route-planning 97
  smartphone 119
  wearable 7
Architectures, service-oriented 31
Artificial intelligence 11, 20, 99, 119, 122, 125, 129, 130, 132
Augmented reality (AR) 122, 129, 130, 133
Automated 51, 86, 91, 92, 129, 130
  decision-making processes 91
  inventory flow 92
  processes 51, 129, 130
  transportation procedures 86
Automatic production 92
Automating tasks 135
Automation 1, 2, 6, 11, 20, 83, 84, 86, 87, 92, 93, 98, 104, 105, 111, 124, 131, 132, 135
  building 1
  home 2, 111
  industrial 20, 87
  robotic procedure 132
  techniques 104
  technologies 104, 131

Automobiles 78
Automotive 9, 119
  dealership 9
  systems 119
Autonomous cars 94

B

Barcode system 131, 132
Battery-operated gadgets 39
Beacons 56, 57, 59, 60, 98, 110
  deploying 57
  in-store bluetooth 110
Billboards 8, 64, 78
  digital 8
  intelligent 78
Bluetooth connectivity 60
Bots, intelligent 55
Brand 56, 67, 70, 76, 79, 97
  ambassadors 56
  development 70
  image 76, 79, 97
  messaging 67
Brand awareness 47, 53
  raising 53
Building automation systems 106
Business(s) 16, 46, 76, 85
  digital marketing 16
  insurance 76
  investments 46
  transport fleets 85

C

CAD software 134
Cloud 24, 29, 40, 83, 124, 125
  computing technologies 83
  infrastructure 24
Cloud-based 61, 96
  database 61
  internet of things 96
Cohesive network 3

Commercial communication systems 5
Communication 3, 4, 20, 21, 23, 27, 28, 40,
    41, 50, 51, 52, 53, 54, 57, 60, 61, 62, 63,
    70, 74, 82, 90, 107, 122
  electronic 107
  global 4
  goal 54
  intelligent 122
  machine 23
  mobile 90
  technology 70, 82
  transmit 57
  verbal 61
  virtual 74
  wireless 52, 61
Components 24, 27, 73
  electronic 27
  environmental 73
  hardware 24
Computer 30, 134, 136
    -aided manufacturing systems 136
    -assisted design (CAD) 134
    -integrated manufacturing (CIM) 30
Computing devices 82
Conditions 27, 86, 88, 92
  factory climate 88
  monitor product 27
  traffic 86, 92
Connections 51, 55, 84, 115, 134
  database 134
  emotional 115
  intelligent 84
  social 55
  web 51
Consumer 15, 16, 24, 30, 52, 98, 119
  connectivity 119
  contexts 24
  data 15, 16, 52
  impression 30
  interactions 98
Consumption 33, 43, 92, 94, 103, 115, 123,
    134
  fuel 94
  water 123
Contemporary security systems 11
Control 14, 24, 29, 47, 93, 94, 95, 103, 111,
    112, 123, 124, 133
  automated 123
  web-based remote 24
Conventional marketing 7, 16, 65, 69

  methods 7, 65
  practices 16, 69
CRM contacts 59
Customer 5, 15, 16, 20, 29, 41, 57
  behavior data 5
  empowerment 29
  privacy 16
  relationship management (CRM) 15, 20,
    41, 57
Customer service 2, 12, 40, 73, 77, 86, 90, 95,
    104, 106, 108, 114, 123
  activities 73
  operations 90
Customer support 1, 63
  services 63
  systems 1

D

Data 28, 51, 77, 91, 115, 122, 125, 129, 131,
    133, 136
  analytics 28, 129, 131, 136
  management 51
  network 133
  sensors 77
  transmission 91, 115, 122
  visualization 125
Data collection 16, 107, 120, 121, 124, 135
  methods 16
  procedure 121
Delivery 9, 12, 20, 25, 32, 57, 62, 73, 85, 93,
    96, 99
  guarantee punctual 93
  system 96
Demands, psychological 23
Deploying IoT-enabled occupancy
    management sensors 88
Deployment of internet of things 15, 52
Devices 3, 4, 8, 11, 24, 39, 50, 51, 56, 57, 60,
    84, 91, 94, 95, 104, 106, 118, 119, 124,
    126, 127, 133
  automated 11, 124
  consumer 106
  deployed 84
  digital 8, 39, 104, 106
  diverse 3, 104
  medical 119
  mobile 24, 56, 57, 60
  networked 127
  wearable 4, 118

Digital 5, 16, 20, 22, 70, 73, 129, 131, 132, 133, 134
    environment 5
    information 73, 133
    marketing tactics 16
    printing technology 134
    technologies 20, 22, 70, 129, 131, 132, 133
Digitalized factory 11
Discourse, contemporary 82
Discovery, continuous 119
Dynamic 42, 48, 59, 75, 76
    pricing 42, 48, 75, 76
    Website Content 59

E

East-west traffic 91
Economic benefits 114
Electrical systems 14
Electromagnetic waves 61
Electronic methods 106
Emotional resonance 103
Energy 83, 85, 111
  consumption 83
  generation 83
  harvesting systems 83
  renewable 83
  solar 83
Enhancing 51, 65, 107, 108
    brand recognition 51
    consumer awareness 65
    customer service 107, 108
Enterprise resource planning (ERP) 94
Environment 8, 13, 28, 54, 69, 111, 130, 133
    contemporary corporate 69
    electronic 54
    operational 28
    virtual 133
Expenses 28, 35, 42, 44, 47, 85, 92, 95, 109
    fuel 92
    managing internal 35

F

Fashion industry 129, 130, 134, 135, 136
    waste statistics 135
Fifth industrial revolution 130
Firm's website 88
Fleet 92
    efficiency 92

management systems 92
Food 25, 29, 77, 87, 89, 112
    package 29
    processing 87
    products 89

G

Gadgets, wireless 59
Global 57, 92, 95, 113
    navigation satellite system (GNSS) 113
    Positioning System (GPS) 57, 92, 95
Google search Ads 56, 57
Governmental laws 72
GPS 59, 86, 92, 95, 113
    cloud-based 86, 92
    navigation systems 59
    trackers 113
    tracking 95

H

Hardware 25, 34, 126
    professionals 25
Healthcare 1, 20, 79
    services 79
    systems 1, 20
Heat maps 110
Home 4, 83
    automation systems 4
    energy management systems 83
Hospitality industry 2
Humidity sensors 89

I

Image recognition techniques 78
Industrial 132, 133
    internet 132, 133
    processes 133
Industries 10, 39, 126, 129, 130, 131, 135
    accessories 131
    automotive 10, 39
    garment 129, 130
    oil 135
    traditional 126
Industry benchmarks 120
Instagram campaigns 73
Instruments 60, 69, 71, 74, 106, 121, 123
    effective 60

technological 106
Integrated marketing communications (IMC) 5, 63
Integration of internet of things 2, 59, 87, 124
Intelligent 11, 14, 27, 39
   device applications 14
   packaging materials 27
   security systems 11
   sensors 39
Interconnected 2, 21, 26, 30, 41, 69, 122, 124
   devices 2, 26, 69, 122, 124
   gadgets 69, 122
   network 21, 41
   systems 30
Internet 50, 57, 104
   -connected devices 104
   landscape 50
   marketing 50, 57
Internet-based 23, 51, 76
   encyclopedia 23
   marketing 76
   technologies 51
Inventory management 11, 28, 77, 88, 93, 95, 98, 99, 100, 123
  procedures 98
  systems 11, 28
  warehouse 100
IoT 3, 13, 14, 15, 16, 19, 20, 21, 23, 24, 25, 31, 34, 35, 39, 44, 45, 46, 47, 51, 60, 61, 62, 74, 79, 80, 83, 93, 96, 108, 109, 118, 119
   adoption 119
   and business model innovation 3
   architecture 31
   commerce 19, 34, 44, 45, 46, 47, 62, 74, 93, 96
   -connected devices 20
   data protocols 51
   devices 13, 14, 21, 24, 39, 51, 118, 119
   machines 35
   product managers 25
   technology 14, 15, 16, 19, 20, 21, 23, 24, 60, 61, 79, 80, 83, 108, 109
IoT application(s) 22, 25, 29, 31, 34, 43, 44, 45, 46, 47, 74, 77
   development 46
   industry 34
IoT-based 30, 47, 79
   penetration pricing system 47
   processing 79

products 30
IoT-enabled 4, 95, 114
   devices 95, 114
   gadgets 4
IoT sensors 28, 94
   contemporary 28

J

Java programming 55

L

Leveraging 43, 74
   IoT technology 43
   sensor warnings 74
Logistics systems 77

M

Machine learning 109, 122, 131, 135
   algorithms 122
Machine-to-infrastructure 23
Machinery 10, 84, 89, 90, 98, 113, 118
   industrial 84, 118
   malfunctioning 89
   failures 90
Machines 13, 65, 130, 132, 134, 135
   automated fabric inspection 132
   coffee 13
   intelligent 130
Marketing 2, 5, 6, 15, 47, 48, 52, 53, 54, 55, 73, 79
   automation 6
   campaign 2, 48, 53, 54
   communications 73
   goals 53
   information 55
   intelligence 79
   reducing 47
   research, augmenting 15, 52
   sensory 5
Mobile phones 54, 113
Monitoring 10, 57, 58, 71, 85, 89, 94, 95, 96, 98, 100, 101, 112, 113, 115, 116, 123, 126
   consumer activity 71
   environmental 85
   traffic 126
Mundane activities 104

N

Nature 72, 121
  competitive 121
  enduring 72
Network 3, 28, 31, 40, 55, 59, 60, 78, 82, 104,
    122, 123, 124, 125, 126, 127, 133, 134
  dynamics 3
  social 55, 78
  traffic 40
Networking 73, 111, 127, 131
  social 73
  wireless 111

O

One-way mass communication 78
Online 22, 36, 42, 75, 76
  bill payment systems 75
  commerce 42
  games 22
  marketing endeavors 75
  newspapers 75
  price sensitivity 76
  stores 36

P

Packaging 26, 28
  food 26
  industry 28
Physical devices 16, 84
Power 15, 39, 44, 112, 121
  consumer bargaining 15
Proactive equipment repair 74
Psychological reactions 105
Public relations professionals 64

R

Renewable energy sources (RESs) 83
RFID technologies 86, 92, 132

S

Seamless transmission 87
Sectors 1, 2, 10, 13, 14, 51, 62, 69, 103, 104,
    106, 130
  automobile 10

construction 13
contemporary business 69, 106
Sensors 24, 26, 29, 39, 44, 74, 76, 77, 78, 83,
    84, 88, 89, 94, 98, 114, 133, 134
  cloud-connected 133
  fitness 78
  remote 133
  video 29
Service(s) 2, 4, 5, 16, 21, 22, 25, 27, 29, 31,
    34, 43, 44, 53, 64, 71, 72, 73, 78, 80, 83,
    106, 120, 121
  demands 34
  firms 73
  guaranteed 25
  providers 43, 44, 78
Signals 59, 132
  advisory warning 132
Significant 6, 10, 16, 50
  data repository 50
  transformations 6, 10, 16, 50
Smart 12, 14, 20, 131, 132
  computing 131
  device applications 14
  grid technology 12
  home applications 20
  manufacturing techniques 132
Software 24, 25, 39, 58, 98, 104, 106, 111,
    126
  applications 106
  technology 98
Supply chain 1, 7, 30, 82, 86, 90, 94, 95, 98,
    131
  management (SCM) 1, 7, 30, 82, 86, 94,
    95, 98, 131
  networks 98
  sourcing 90

T

Tailored 56, 59
  advertising techniques 56
  target segments 59
Target audience 5, 7, 22, 53, 57, 60, 64, 66,
    69, 70, 91, 92, 120
Technologies 14, 54, 99, 122, 131
  sensor 131
  smart 54
  transformative 14
  warehouse 99
  wearable 122

Textile mills 135
Transformation 12, 16, 30, 36, 72, 75, 83, 94,
    103, 104, 115
  digital 72
  organic 36
Transportation methods 93

V

Vehicles 9, 10, 72, 76, 78, 94, 126
  autonomous 94
Virtual reality (VR) 129, 130, 131, 133

W

Wastage, reducing 9, 93
Waste, reducing 92, 134
Wearables, embedded 12
WiFi 9, 110
    network 9
    signals 110
Wireless 20, 21, 53, 74, 76, 106
    networking technologies 76
    networks 20, 53, 74
    sensor networks 21, 106

www.ingramcontent.com/pod-product-compliance
Lightning Source LLC
Chambersburg PA
CBHW041444210326
41599CB00004B/122